About Christian

Margaret and David C. Ekstrand

To order additional copies of this book, contact:
Xlibris
844-714-8691
www.Xlibris.com
Orders@Xlibris.com

ISBN: Softcover   978-1-6641-9051-1
        EBook   978-1-6641-9050-4

Print information available on the last page

Rev. date: 08/18/2021

CONTENTS

For our children both here and in heaven

PREFACE

Testimony: a solemn statement made under oath, an assertion offering firsthand authentication of a fact; something that serves as evidence.

This is our testimony, but our hope is that it will be Christian's testimony when he grows up. During the first year of his life, we used email to update our friends and family on Christian's progress. At the same time, Margaret kept a journal to communicate her prayers to God. For us, writing was the best way to express our fears, praise, frustration, and hope. We hope it presents an accurate picture of the events in Christian's first year.

In this book, *the boys* refer to our two older sons, Brenton, who was nine years old when Christian was born, and Jordan, who was six. Their story is reflected in this work, as well.

CHAPTER 1
Birth to Five Days

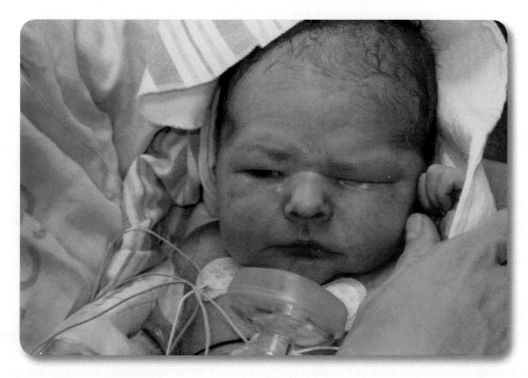

Friday, April 25, 2003, 11:18 PM

Hi all,

Well, I am running on very little sleep as I write this (almost 11:00 PM Friday, I think), but I wanted to give everyone an update on our new son.

His name is Christian Elias Ekstrand and he was born on Thursday, April 24 at 10:24 AM. He weighed in at 9 pounds, 9 ounces, and measured 22.5 inches long. Mom is doing pretty well after lengthy labor. You can find pictures of Mom and Sweet Pea (as we call him) on our website.

Shortly after Christian was born, the nurse noticed that he was having difficulty breathing and suggested that he be checked out. After about two hours of poking and prodding, it was discovered that his heart was enlarged. The cardiologist suggested that he be transferred to Stanford Children's Hospital immediately.

At Stanford this morning, doctors used a catheter to do some more investigation and discovered that the valves to and from the left ventricle are too small, which means the chamber is unable to handle the pumping work of the heart. The doctors used the catheter to insert a connector between the left and right atriums, which will cause the right ventricle to take some of the load off the left ventricle. This solution, however, is temporary and he will be requiring surgery by next week.

Margaret and I would appreciate any prayers you could offer on Christian's behalf. The doctors say he is strong and has been responding well to his treatments. It is difficult for us to be separated from him so much, but we know that he is receiving good care. More difficult for us is to give up our little Sweet Pea to God. We trust that God is in control and has a plan for our little boy.

Thank you for all your prayers, support, and love. God's blessings on you all.

Cheers.

 Margaret's Journal

Dear Lord,

On Thursday, April 24, 2003, at 10:24 AM, Christian Elias Ekstrand was born. For over ten nights, I had labor pains after 9:00 PM. Every night, I thought we'd be rushing to the hospital. Because I expected a very fast delivery, I was concerned that David might be at work and miss the delivery. Thankfully, David was able to work at home for the few weeks before the due date. I thought the baby would come after the OB doctor irritated my cervix on April 18. I was bleeding for a few days and had painful contractions.

On April 15, we celebrated David's thirty-sixth birthday with his parents and then came to the house for dessert. The next evening was the full moon and still the baby didn't come. By Easter, I was really surprised that our baby had not arrived yet. I really thought we would miss church on Easter Sunday. I was so huge and looked so pregnant (at 173 pounds). I gained a total of thirty-three or thirty-four pounds. We went to church on Easter and it was a beautiful Sunday. I remember it was very relaxing and peaceful. The boys brought flowers to put on the cross for Jesus. After church, we went to Dana and Mike's (David's parents) for Easter dinner.

Christian's birthday finally came on Thursday the twenty-fourth. It began at about 1:20 AM. I felt a few major contractions then I fell back to sleep. I felt more at 2:00 AM. At 3:00 AM, I woke up with stronger, regular contractions. We both got up and got ready. David pulled the van into the driveway. I got dressed to go. We called Mike and Dana. Everything went really smoothly. There was no panic or emergency. We were ready and calm. When Mike arrived, I walked out to the van. Grampa Mike stayed with the boys while we went to the hospital.

We arrived at San Jose Regional Medical Center at 4:00 AM. I had only one really big contraction on the way there. The hospital wasn't crowded that night. I remember we called my OB, Dr. Gretkowski, on the way to the hospital. She said she would be there soon. It was much later when she arrived. I was only 4 cm dilated so I took a small pain reliever (Stadol). It wasn't very helpful. I remember seeing stars and the room became quieter. I could not clearly hear what people were saying. All the pain for each contraction was still there. David was a wonderful coach and helped me to breathe through each contraction.

About 8:00 AM, Dr. Gretkowski arrived and I felt like I was going to have the baby any minute. She said she would come back when I was more dilated. It was so painful when they checked to see if I was dilated while in labor. Yikes! One nurse was very rough. Nurse Julie was especially good. We praise God for her. She had to tell me the news there might be complications with Christian.

After more pushes than I can count and more pain than I ever want to remember, baby Sweet Pea was born. They let me hold him on my chest for a minute before they cleaned him up. I did not hear a really loud cry ever. They wrapped him and I held him in my arms with David next to me. I wish I could have held him all day. I was weak and needed stitches so I let David hold him while they were sewing me up. David was admiring him and holding him. We still had not named him. The nurse said they needed to check his oxygen level. His color was not good, so they gave him oxygen. I went to the recovery room and David watched the nurses care for the baby for hours.

I checked into my room and they brought me some dinner. I missed the baby and I asked David to take me in a wheelchair to see him. Praise God I did that. I wish it had been sooner. I was able to be with him for one hour and hold him for a few minutes. We took some pictures, of course. Then the cardiologist came and did an ultrasound on Christian's heart. This was the beginning of discovering his heart problems. They said he needed to be transported to Stanford Children's Hospital (Lucile Packard Children's Hospital at Stanford).

I was in shock. I just wanted to hold him there. I couldn't imagine it was so serious. He didn't look bad. He looked beautiful! I thought maybe they could let me hold him and nurse him until morning. I thought that would be best. Instead, they set up a transport for him to leave that night.

They brought my baby to see me at about 11:00 PM. They needed to know if we had named him yet. It was a very emotional and difficult time. On that day, April 24, 2003, we named him Christian Elias Ekstrand. David and I did not want him to be Baby Boy Ekstrand. David left my side and went to be with Christian all night.

Our little boy Christian Elias is so big. He is 9 pounds, 9 ounces, and 22 1/2 inches long—the biggest of my three baby boys.

Saturday, April 26, 2003, 10:42 PM

Good evening all,

I just want to start by saying that God is a good God. His strength and mercy through His Son Jesus Christ and by the work of the Holy Spirit have sustained us since the birth of our son. We trust in His sovereignty and in His grace during this time.

Next, I would like to thank all of you for your prayers, for your words of encouragement and empathy, and for the love you have shown our family. What a blessing to have friends and family that love us so much. We thank God for all of you and ask for His blessing on each of you and your families.

So here is the update.

Christian's left ventricle (the pump that sends blood to the body through the aorta) is definitely not working. To solve the problem, the doctors at Packard Children's Hospital want to start working on his heart as soon as possible. Starting on Monday at 10:00 AM, he will have the first of three surgeries to essentially transfer the work of the left ventricle to the right ventricle (the pump that usually just sends blood to the lungs). This first surgery will directly connect the right ventricle to both the aorta and the lungs. Because this will mix oxygenated blood with unoxygenated blood, he will have a pale blue tint for a while. This surgery will hold him until he is three to six months old.

The surgery at three to six months will take him a step closer to the final surgery that he will need at one to four years old. The last surgery will reconfigure his system so that the blood flows from the body to the lungs and then to the heart.

Things you can pray for:

- Ask God to heal Christian.
- Christian has a blood clot in his left leg. This is a result of the catheter the doctors used to investigate the heart. They want to make sure that it is cleared up before they perform surgery on Monday. Ask that God would heal his leg.
- The surgery Christian will be having on Monday is major and has a great deal of associated risks. Pray that God would grant the surgeon and his team wisdom and skill as they perform the surgery, monitor his vitals, and solve any problems they may encounter.
- Recovery from this surgery can take anywhere from ten days to a month. Pray that Christian's recovery will be thorough and quick.
- The emotional and physical stress of not being able to nurse her new baby is weighing heavy on Margaret. Pray that she would be able to produce and store enough milk for when Christian is able to start taking it.

Again, thank you all for your love and prayers.
In Christ's loving hands,
DCE

Sunday, April 27, 2003, 12:06 PM

Good morning,

In the midst of all of our requests, I wanted to take the time to offer praises to our Father in heaven.

- Praise God that He chose to expand our family and entrust us with this gift of another son.
- Praise God that Margaret was able to deliver Christian with minimal complications.
- Praise God that our delivery nurse, Julie, noticed right away that Christian's breathing was not right. This quick action probably saved his life.
- Praise God for Anita, the nursery nurse at Regional Medical Center, who worked an extra shift to make sure Christian was ready for transport to Stanford.
- Praise God that Margaret and I were able to hold Christian before he was put on a ventilator and transported to Stanford.
- Praise God that we live close to one of the world's best children's hospitals, specifically equipped to deal with cardiac problems.
- Praise God for medical insurance.
- Praise God for Dr. Stevenson, Dr. Perry, and Dr. Feinstein and for their wisdom in evaluating and identifying the issue with Christian's heart.
- Praise God for Nancy and the other nurses that are caring for Christian in the NICU at Stanford.
- Praise God that both of our families are close and able to offer so much support. Some of the other babies in the NICU are from other parts of the world and the parents are often without a support system.
- Praise God for our friends who have been so giving in both physical, emotional, and spiritual support. We are blessed to have them.
- Praise God for His faithfulness and His complete control.

2 Chronicles 16:9 says, "For the eyes of the Lord move to and fro throughout the earth that He may strongly support those whose heart is completely His." We are experiencing His strong support as we strive to make our hearts completely His.

Continue to pray for Christian's healing. The blood clot in his left leg still has not cleared. We are asking that God would directly intervene to heal his leg.

God bless you all and keep you in His care.

DCE

Sunday, April 27, 2003, 11:39 PM

All,

As a quick update, we are waiting to find out whether or not Christian will go into surgery tomorrow (Monday). The blood clot in his left leg will be reevaluated to see if surgery should be postponed to clear it up. Right now, we wait for his leg to improve, and we pray that the doctors will show wisdom and skill as they make decisions on Christian's care.

Again, we thank you for your phone calls, gifts, emails, and other support. I apologize for not getting back to each of you immediately, but please know that we appreciate all your support.

God bless you all.

DCE

Monday, April 28, 2003, 8:06 AM

All,

Praise God! The blood clot in Christian's leg has cleared and he has been taken off some of the medications. This means he will probably go into surgery at 10:00 AM (PST) this morning.

Please ask for God's protection as Christian goes into surgery. Ask for God's wisdom for the surgeons as they work on Christian. Ask that God would grant us peace that surpasses all understanding on this day.

God's blessings on you all and our thanks for your support and love.

DCE

Monday, April 28, 2003, 8:49 PM

> To Thee, O Lord, I call; my rock, do not be deaf to me, lest if Thou are silent to me, I become like those who go down to the pit. Hear the voice of my supplications when I cry to Thee for help, when I lift up my hands toward Thy holy sanctuary. (Psalm 28:1–2)

Today has been full of uncertainty and frustration. We were expecting Christian to go into surgery today at 10:00 AM but did not find out until after 1:00 PM that his surgery will be tomorrow morning (at 10:00 AM). My frustration is not with the care he has been receiving—it has been excellent. My frustration is in my inability to control the situation. I have not been at peace today.

We spoke with the surgeon this afternoon to get the details of the surgery. It was good to see the face of the doctor I will be praying for. The surgery will last approximately six hours from the time he goes into the operating room to the time he goes into recovery at the cardio-vascular intensive care unit (CVICU). The doctor feels that Christian's chances are good that he will get through this operation. Nevertheless, we ask that you continue to pray for his safety.

Margaret is doing a little better today. She is still recovering from the birth, and she still needs lots of rest. The emotional stress of not having Christian home with us is wearing on her. It was nice, however, to have Brenton and Jordan home with us last night and all day today.

As Christian goes into surgery tomorrow, please keep him in your prayers. Also, pray for Dr. Reddy and his surgical team that God would grant them an extra measure of wisdom and skill as they work on Christian. Most of all, ask that God's power, grace, and sovereignty would be seen in this situation. In spite of my frustrations, I continue to trust that Jesus is Lord and Jesus is present.

> Blessed be the Lord, Because He has heard the voice of my supplication. The Lord is my strength and my shield; My heart trusts in Him, and I am helped; Therefore my heart exults, And with my song I shall thank Him. (Psalm 28:6–7)

God's blessings on you all.

DCE

CHAPTER 2
First Surgery and Recovery

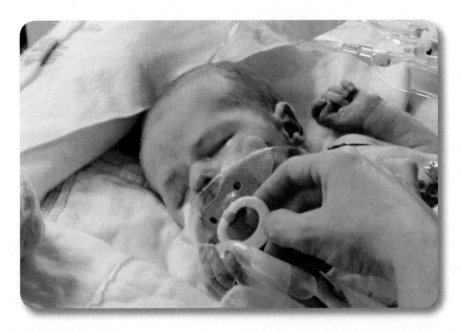

Tuesday, April 29, 2003, 10:34 PM

All,

Christian was taken into surgery this morning at 11:15 AM. Margaret and I got to spend some time with him before he went in, and he was quite alert (considering how medicated he was). At 5:30 PM, the surgeon, Dr. Reddy, informed us that the surgery went well. They completed the procedure to connect his pulmonary arteries to his aorta and (as a bonus) salvaged the valves on the left ventricle, giving the surgeons more options down the road.

We were able to see him about an hour later in the CVICU and he looks pretty good. He has a lot of tubes going into and out of his body, his wound is still open (until Friday), and he is really sedated. But it was wonderful to see him and touch his head and praise God for His mercy.

Thank you, all, for your prayers. Thank you for your support and care. Thank you for standing with us and interceding on our behalf before a gracious and powerful God through His Son, Jesus Christ.

> Ascribe to the Lord, O sons of the mighty, Ascribe to the Lord glory and strength. Ascribe to the Lord the glory due to His name; Worship the Lord in holy array! (Psalm 29:1–2)

Ascribe greatness to the Lord on high!
In God's hands,
DCE

Wednesday, April 30, 2003, 10:51 PM

All,

> Trust in the Lord with all your heart, And do not lean on your own understanding. In all your ways acknowledge Him, And He will make your paths straight. (Prov. 3:5–6)

Margaret and I are asking God to make our paths straight. Today begins a long road of recovery for Christian. We called several times last night and early this morning to check on him and each time it was reported that he was stable. The surgeon made his rounds and was confident that he would be closing up Christian's chest on Friday, a very good sign that his recovery is going well. We praise God for His healing mercies on little Christian.

Some of the information on Christian's recovery was difficult for Margaret to hear. Since he has never been nursed, he will need to learn how to swallow and suck. Because it will be so long after his birth, it may take some time for him to learn these skills and there may be a long delay before he is able to nurse, something Margaret was looking forward to as a way to bond with her new baby boy. Please pray on Margaret's behalf that she would be comforted.

Our family has received many blessings from our friends and family. Many have offered to provide meals, to watch our kids, to teach our kids (they are normally schooled at home), to sit with us as we wait in the hospital, to research our child's heart condition and share the information with us, or to take time to pray for us and with us. The Apostle Paul told his friends in the church at Phillipi that "you have done well to share with me in my affliction." I would like to echo that praise. You have shared so much with us and we are grateful.

Please continue to lift up Christian in your prayers. Ask that God would restore his health and protect him from any affliction. Pray for the medical staff that is attending to him, that they would use wisdom and their experience to provide him with the best possible care. And please ask God to prepare Margaret, Brenton, Jordan, and me for whatever lies ahead—that we would have the grace and faith to embrace God's plan for Christian.

God grant you peace and grace as you go through your days and nights.

Cheers.

DCE

Thursday, May 1, 2003, 11:26 PM

All,

I will be making this short as I am just exhausted today. Christian remains stable and there is a good chance that the doctors will close his chest tomorrow. We thank God for his healing mercies on Christian and we continue to praise Him for this wonderful gift he has entrusted us with.

Please continue to pray for Christian. Around 7:00 PM tonight, his monitors recorded an arrhythmia (irregular heartbeat) possibly due to a premature atrial contraction (the heart might have pumped before the atrium was completely full). We spoke with the nurse and she indicated that this will be monitored and might be due to the placement of the electrodes that sense the heartbeat. We are asking God to give Christian a regular, stable heartbeat.

Grateful for God's mercies and submissive to His will,

DCE

Friday, May 2, 2003, 10:11 AM

> Why are you in despair, O my soul? And why have you become disturbed within me? Hope in God, for I shall again praise Him For the help of His presence. (Psalm 42:5)

All,

I had an opportunity to correspond with a student at Stanford this morning. He had written an article in the school newspaper about "the religion thing" and was talking about his investigation of Christianity. As

I wrote to him, it was a good reminder that I don't depend on religion but on a relationship with the perfect Creator of the universe, a relationship that He instigated and provided for through His Son, Jesus Christ. I know that it is this relationship which sustains me and sustains Margaret. Without it, we would not only be lost for eternity but lost in the present. We thank God for the help of His presence.

The hospital staff told us that the surgeon, Dr. Reddy, would be closing up Christian's chest at noon today. They will actually do the procedure at his bed, rather than move him to an operating room. They will bring the OR team in and create a sterile environment right in the CVICU. Please pray that God would grant Dr. Reddy and his team wisdom as they assess Christian's condition and grant them skill as they carry out the procedure. We continue to pray for Christian's recovery and recognize that we have witnessed miracle after miracle in the past seven days. We don't take them for granted anymore.

God bless you and keep you and may you experience His presence.

Cheers.

DCE

Friday, May 2, 2003, 10:49 PM

> I will sing of the mercies of the Lord forever: with my mouth will I make known thy faithfulness to
> all generations. (Psalm 89:1, KJV)

Today has been a good day. The procedure to close Christian's chest went very well. Furthermore, the doctors have begun the lengthy process of making him less reliant on the ventilator. The surgeon checked in on him several times today and had only positive things to say. The doctors and nurses think he is progressing nicely.

But the best part was that Christian opened his eyes for about ten minutes today. Margaret and I chatted away with him as he looked at his surroundings. We hadn't seen him open his eyes since Tuesday, so this was very exciting. To cap off this great day, members of our small group brought dinner and company. They are such a blessing to us.

Please continue to ask God to give the hospital staff wisdom as they constantly evaluate Christian's condition. Also, ask that God would use us to be a blessing and witness to them of the love and grace of God through His Son, Jesus Christ.

On a day like this, it is easy for me to sing of God's mercies. Pray that I will be able to sing of His mercies even on the bad days.

God's Spirit watch over you and yours.

Cheers.

DCE

Saturday, May 3, 2003, 8:53 AM

All,

My dad has not been feeling well since he spent a couple of days at the hospital with Christian and me. We thought it was just an upset stomach or fatigue. He saw his doctor a few times last week and last night they discovered that his appendix had perforated. He had surgery at 1:00 AM this morning and is now recovering. Please pray for his full recovery. As many of you know, I just went through this same thing last September, and my recovery was pretty rough. My dad is (obviously) older than me and is diabetic, so it will be a lot more difficult for him.

Thank you for your support and prayer.

God bless.

DCE

CHAPTER 3
Through the Valley

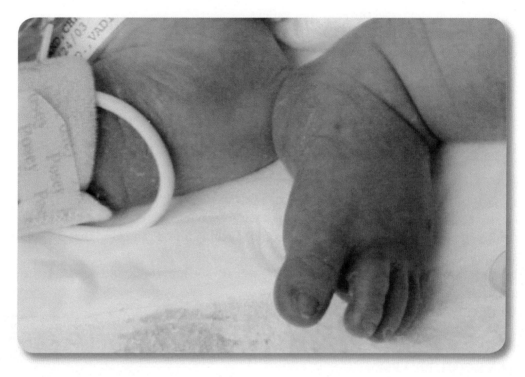

Saturday, May 3, 2003, 11:49 PM

Friends,

I have always loved the twenty-third Psalm. For as long as I can remember, the imagery has always allowed me to make God a little more tangible. As I have grown older and gone through different events, I find more truth in the words of the psalmist:

> Even though I walk through the valley of the shadow of death, I fear no evil; for Thou art with me;
> Thy rod and Thy staff, they comfort me.

It is interesting to note that God does not steer us around the valleys we encounter. Instead, He promises His presence and His comfort as we go through them.

It has been an emotional day and we feel we are getting deeper and deeper into this valley. We see our expectations of a quick recovery, of being able to cradle Christian in our arms, of hearing him cry, and yes, even of changing his dirty diaper, being pushed further and further away and the thought of those unmet expectations is becoming overwhelming. We had hopes of seeing further progress with Christian today. Instead, the nurses and doctors spent most of the day trying to deal with his increased heart rate. The feelings of helplessness are beginning to take their toll. Please pray that we will find hope and strength even as we pray that our little one will be strengthened. Ask that God would send His Holy Spirit to bring peace and comfort to Christian as he endures this slow process of healing.

I spoke with my father today and he is doing well, considering he just had an appendectomy. While his appendix perforated some time ago (they think as far back as three days ago), it was contained and did not spread to his abdomen. This is a real blessing and we anticipate a quick recovery. Please ask for God to heal him and allow him to return home soon.

> Now to Him who is able to do exceeding abundantly beyond all that we ask or think, according to the power that works within us, to Him be the glory in the church and in Christ Jesus to all generations forever and ever. Amen. (Eph. 3:20–21)

God be with you as you travel through your valleys.
In His merciful care,
David and family

Monday, May 5, 2003, 12:45 AM

Friends,

Margaret and I are so thankful for your emails and phone calls. It is very encouraging to know that so many of you are praying for us. Thank you also for the wise advice and offers of support. We couldn't be in better hands—God's hands working through people.

Quick update on two fronts. First of all, Christian was stable all day. His heart rate was much better today and as an added bonus, the drainage tubes from his chest were removed. We even got to hold his hand today. We spent much of the day with him, talking to him and touching him. Praise God that we were able to spend so much time with him.

On the second front, my father is doing well. We went to see him today and he expects to be home this week. Praise God for healing Dad.

God bless you.
DCE

Monday, May 5, 2003, 10:13 PM

> Praise be to the God and Father of our Lord Jesus Christ, the Father of compassion and the God of all comfort, who comforts us in all our troubles, so that we can comfort those in any trouble with the comfort we ourselves have received from God. (2 Cor. 1:3–4, NIV)

Wow, what a promise! To know that I belong to a compassionate and comforting God allows me to face each day with hope. It is amazing to see how God meets our need for comfort and compassion through His Holy Spirit and through other people. And as Rick Warren (pastor of Saddleback Church) says, "God never wastes a hurt." We know that what we are going through now will allow us to empathize with and comfort others. Praise God for His plan.

Christian made progress today. The saying among the CVICU parents is "Baby steps, always baby steps." It's a reminder that even a little progress is still progress. Today Christian was able to be taken off two medications. His heart rate is at a good level and his blood pressure is stable. These are all good signs and bring us just that much closer to a time when we can hold him in our arms. Speaking of arms, please pray that God will heal his right arm. He had to have it taped in an uncomfortable position to allow for an IV since Tuesday. They unwrapped it today and it wasn't in great shape and it really hurts him to touch or move it. He is already pretty uncomfortable. Ask that God would have His hand on Christian's arm.

Margaret spent most of the day with Brenton and Jordan, going over their lessons and taking them to some extracurricular activities. It was hard for her to not be at the hospital, but the boys were glad to spend some time with Mom. Please continue to pray that the two of them will be flexible and sympathetic as we attend to Christian.

As for my father, he is recovering and may get to come home tomorrow. Please ask that God would comfort him, as well. He is lonely being in the hospital and really needs to be home.

Once again, I want to thank so many of you for your love and encouragement. It is a blessing to read your emails and cards and spend time with some of you. Know that God is using you to minister to our family.

May you experience God's peace in your daily journey.

Clinging to Christ,

DCE

Tuesday, May 6, 2003, 9:58 PM

> And we rejoice in the hope of the glory of God. Not only so, but we also rejoice in our sufferings, because we know that suffering produces perseverance; perseverance, character; and character, hope. And hope does not disappoint us, because God has poured out His love into our hearts by the Holy Spirit, who He has given us. (Rom. 5:2–5, NIV)

Margaret commented today that the last week or so feels like a marathon. I have never participated in a marathon, partly because of my asthma and partly because they have never interested me. A marathon takes endurance—something I tend to be short on. When I look at what Paul had to say to the church in Rome, I see myself just trying to deal with perseverance. Will I hold to this course long enough to produce character? Am I able to see this hope that does not disappoint? These are just some of the questions that Margaret and I are dealing with right now.

Christian has remained stable since yesterday but still faces challenges. The road to independence from the medications and machines he is connected to is a long one. He had to be put back on one of the medications today because his blood pressure dropped a little too low. He is also receiving more blood to keep his blood pressure up. It seems for every couple of steps forward we take a step back. The hope of holding Christian in our arms still seems distant. Please pray that Christian will continue healing and that we will be able to endure this trial.

Doctors also discovered a bacterial infection in Christian. They started him on a general antibiotic until they identify the specific bacteria. The nurses have said that he will probably experience some flu-like symptoms as his body fights the infection. He is already pretty uncomfortable so this is difficult for us to hear. His right arm is still not in good shape, and they had to put another IV in it today. Since he cannot cry with the intubation tube, he often makes a *scrunchy face* when he is uncomfortable or unhappy. He has been making this face a lot. Please pray that the Holy Spirit will bring peace and comfort to Christian's little body.

As praise, my father got to go home today. He and my mother are very relieved, and he is a lot more relaxed. Pray that God would make his recovery complete and that his mind would be at peace.

To those of you who have given your time and energy to minister to our family, thank you. You are truly a blessing. May God grant you His peace and comfort.

Looking to the hope that does not disappoint,

DCE

Wednesday, May 7, 2003, 11:38 PM

> So we're not giving up. How could we! Even though on the outside it often looks like things are falling apart on us, on the inside, where God is making new life, not a day goes by without his unfolding grace. These hard times are small potatoes compared to the coming good times, the lavish celebration

prepared for us. There's far more here than meets the eye. The things we see now are here today, gone tomorrow. But the things we can't see now will last forever. (2 Cor. 4:16–18, The Message)

When you are in the midst of a hard time, it is difficult to think of it as *small potatoes,* but the promise we cling to is His grace. We also know that the hard time is probably necessary for us to even experience His grace and to see something God-glorifying built up in us. Just like Christian must go through great pain to get his heart working properly, God often has to subject us to great pain to change the condition of our character. And the reward will far outweigh whatever pain we may have encountered here. God made us a promise. Pray for God's mercy as He shapes our character.

Christian continues to recover. He was able to stay off one of his medications today and still keep his blood pressure up. This is a real blessing. And he got some food through his NG tube (for those of you who don't know, this tube goes up the nose and into the stomach, so he probably isn't enjoying it much). At first they gave him some formula, but after Margaret let the staff know that she wasn't pumping breast milk for two weeks as a hobby, they admitted their mistake and started Christian on her milk. Right now, the doctors are watching how well he digests the milk and are monitoring his body temperature. They are also continuing to check for bacteria (he is still coming up negative, but the doctors want to make sure) and are trying to help him get rid of the excess fluid in his body. Please pray that Christian will not have any problems with his stomach or with his body temperature.

It was such a blessing to see his eyes today. We spent an hour or so talking to him and watching him try to track sounds with his eyes. He has beautiful eyes and is very expressive with them.

Thank you for your continued prayer and for your acts of blessing on our family. May God continue to grant you peace.

Experiencing God's unfolding grace,
DCE

Thursday, May 8, 2003, 10:50 AM

Friends,
This morning, the doctors started the process that will ultimately take Christian off the respirator. He is already at the lowest rate for the respirator, and he is doing a lot of the breathing on his own. They discontinued the milk through his NG tube and will be taking x-rays of his chest. If the x-rays look good, they will take him off the respirator and extubate him (take the tube out of his windpipe). This is another step closer to his full recovery. Please pray that the doctors would have wisdom as they evaluate him and that Christian would be able to breathe on his own without assistance.

Thank you for your prayers.
Cheers.
DCE

Thursday, May 8, 2003, 10:12 PM

Friends,
I would like to make something clear. Please do not get the impression that I have somehow figured things out. I have not. My hope is that someday I can, by God's grace, look back on this and see how God has shaped me and my family and how things were brought about to bring God glory. But right now, I'm am still full of questions and uncertainty. One thing that has been a great blessing is hearing how God has brought you through similar trials. It is encouraging for us to read and listen to your own stories from the other end of that journey. Thanks for sharing with us.

In the twelfth chapter of Paul's second letter to the church in Corinth, Paul spends some time talking about weakness. After asking God three times to take away an affliction, God answers Paul with these words, "My grace is sufficient for you, for My power is made perfect in weakness" (2 Cor. 12:9, NIV).

I will admit right now that I am weak. The emotional and physical drain is beginning to take its toll. The strain on my faith is beginning to show, as well. Despite this, I believe God's promise to Paul is also offered to us. First, God will provide His goodwill and mercy, enough to get us through that particular trial. Second, He promises that our weakness will bring about our full development according to His specific plan for us. Not only does He promise the end result, but also promises us a way to get there—by His grace. These are promises that we are living by right now.

We want to thank God for the care the Christian has been receiving at Lucile Packard Children's Hospital. We have been blessed with caring, competent nurses, skilled doctors, and good support staff. Today we had good reason to be thankful for their work. The plan was to take Christian off the respirator, but after noting from the x-rays the lungs were not completely inflated, the plan was delayed. Instead, they had a respiratory therapist work with Christian to get the lungs expanded. They also did a test to see if he could breathe on his own if the respirator was set to zero. He passed the test and they are planning to take him off and extubate him tomorrow morning. Please pray that he continues to show signs that he is ready for this.

Also, please pray for continued healing for Christian. Today, they had to remove an IV line because it was severely irritating his abdomen. Because he has had so many IVs, it is difficult to find a new place to put one in. They decided (after poking him a few times) that he didn't need a second IV and that he could probably come off another medication. This is a mixed blessing but a blessing nonetheless. Furthermore, his arm has not completely healed from the IV that was removed a couple of days ago. Not only will he need to heal from the heart surgery, but he will also need to heal from the recovery.

In the name of Jesus Christ, God's Son, may God richly bless you and give you peace by the power of His Holy Spirit.

In His grace,

DCE

Friday, May 9, 2003, 10:44 PM

Today was very exhausting for Margaret and me. Part of the problem is our expectations. We were hoping to see Christian off of his respirator and a little more active today. However, when we got to the hospital, we were told that it may be a couple more days before that happens so that Christian's lungs can clear out some of the fluid in them.

The other part of the problem is the amount of information we have readily available. Monitors track his heart rate, blood pressure, oxygen saturation in his blood, rate of breathing, temperature, and so on. Any time something changes, an alarm sounds or a light flashes. Whenever that happens, we hold our breath, waiting to see if this is serious or just a fluctuation. It has become nerve-racking for me. While Margaret is at peace being at Christian's side, I find myself so tightly wound that I can hardly stand it.

We are both feeling the effects of the emotional drain. Every time he has to have another IV put in, or has to have his equipment rearranged, we can see the discomfort in his face. While we know he will probably not remember any of this, it is still hard for us to watch.

Despite this, we are thankful for his improvements. He is stable. He is still being fed Margaret's milk and is digesting it. He was taken off another medication last night. He has caring nurses watching over him and wise doctors helping him to recover.

The words of Jesus keep running through my head:

> Come to me, all you who are weary and burdened, and I will give you rest. Take my yoke upon you and learn from me, for I am gentle and humble in heart, and you will find rest for your souls. For my yoke is easy and my burden is light. (Matt. 11:28–30, NIV)

We are weary and burdened, but we know Jesus is gentle. We know Jesus is Lord and accept the burden He places on us. Finally, we know we are not alone, for this yoke and burden are His. He carries it alongside us. Thank you, Jesus.

Thank you all for your prayer and for your help. God bless you richly.

In Christ,

DCE

Saturday, May 10, 2003, 10:24 PM

Today has been the most difficult day of my life. On the one hand, you could say that I have had a very easy life—and you would be correct. On the other hand, I also know that there are difficult days ahead. It was challenging for me to watch my son, Christian, struggle to breathe after being extubated. And it was heartbreaking to hear the doctor say that Christian would have to be intubated again and put back on the respirator. It will be two or three days before the doctors try to extubate him again. Until then, we must wait for him to get stronger.

Oh Lord, give us peace and give comfort to Christian. Amen.

DCE

Sunday, May 11, 2003, 10:21 PM

Friends,

It is amazing what expectations will do. Margaret and I went to bed last night exhausted and in tears. We cried out to God for peace and comfort and He was merciful. Today, we just didn't set our expectations so high. Instead, we planned to listen to Brenton and Jordan sing at church to celebrate Mother's Day. We received wise teaching from our pastor and love from our friends. It was a great start to the day.

Throughout the night and into the morning, we had been calling Christian's nurse for updates and were pleased to hear that the night was uneventful. When we went to see him this afternoon, he was sleeping peacefully. We didn't expect much to happen, but it was a blessing to see that he was taking more breast milk (20 cc/hour). This is important because it will help strengthen his body. He also had both his foley catheter (you'll just have to look that one up on your own) and his abdominal drain tube removed. This is important because it greatly decreases his chances of getting an infection. He slept throughout the afternoon, and we were able to touch him and talk to him. It was a peaceful day for us.

We thank God for His blessings of mercy, peace, and comfort. We thank Him for the people He has put in our lives to minister to us, to disciple us, and to support us. We praise Him for the work that He has done in our lives and thank Him for the gifts of our sons. While submitting to His will, we ask God for complete healing of Christian's heart and give Him glory for whatever work He will perform through us, in us, and about us. We echo the prayer of David and say,

> May God be gracious to us and bless us and make his face shine upon us, that your ways may be known on earth, your salvation among all nations.
>
> May the peoples praise you, O God; may all the peoples praise you. May the nations be glad and sing for joy, for you rule the peoples justly and guide the nations of the earth. May the peoples praise you, O God; may all the peoples praise you.
>
> Then the land will yield its harvest, and God, our God, will bless us. God will bless us, and all the ends of the earth will fear him. (Psalm 67, NIV)

Amen.

Again, I want to thank you for your prayers, your support, your emails, and phone calls and for your willing ministry to our family. God bless and keep you.

DCE

Tuesday, May 13, 2003, 12:21 AM

Friends,

God continues to extend His healing mercies to Christian. Today, he remained stable and continues to *fatten up*. The doctors have increased his calorie intake and continue to try to reduce the amount of fluid in his lungs. These two things are necessary for successful extubation.

The doctors are also treating a minor infection (conjunctivitis) in his eyes but have taken him off his blood pressure medicine. They also lowered his dosage of sedatives. This made him more alert today, so he and I had a little chat about life, sport, girls, etc.,—you know, guy things. I sang a little to him and let him track his stuffed bear with his eyes (pretty tricky, if you cannot move your head). After about half an hour of that, he fell asleep again and has been pretty peaceful.

We praise God for the improvements that we have seen. We praise Him for the wisdom and skill He has given to the doctors and nurses. We praise Him for the testimony of His faithfulness that has been seen in this event. And we continue to make our requests for a complete recovery known to God.

Thank you for your prayers and for your ministry to our family. We are blessed.

> The grace of the Lord Jesus Christ, and the love of God, and the fellowship of the Holy Spirit, be with you all. (2 Cor. 13:14)

Gratefully,
DCE

Wednesday, May 14, 2003, 12:33 AM

One of the nurses shared a lesson learned by another family that went through the same heart surgeries we are going through. The mother in that family commented, "After the first surgery, I discovered that recovery is like a roller coaster . . . and I fought that roller coaster the entire time. When we went into the second surgery, I decided just to ride the roller coaster."

Today was a dip in the roller coaster. When we arrived at the hospital today, we were told that Christian would be extubated and taken off the respirator. His milk was discontinued and his sedatives/pain medications were reduced. The plan was to extubate him at 4:00 PM, but the doctors continued to monitor his lungs and strength until they were satisfied with the results. It was about two hours later that he was removed from the respirator and allowed to breathe on his own. Since his vocal cords were raw from having the tube in his windpipe, he cried quite a bit but was too hoarse to be heard. He did, however, settle down when given a pacifier. It was a great blessing that he was able to suck on the pacifier as this was a skill he had never used before.

After about a half-hour, the nurse noticed that he was not getting rid of the CO_2 as he should. The doctors put him on a C-PAP, which is a device that forces air pressure into the nose and down to the windpipe. It was hoped that this would trigger his body to take bigger breathes and push out the CO_2. However, this did not prove successful and after being off the respirator for nearly an hour, he was sedated and intubated again. While he did not look uncomfortable like the last time he was extubated, it was becoming apparent that the CO_2 levels in his blood were getting dangerous.

We were able to spend a little time with him without a tube in his mouth. We took some pictures and let him practice sucking on the pacifier. He has a beautiful mouth and a nice pout.

We are a little down tonight and we are pondering in our mind why he is not yet strong enough to breathe on his own. The doctors have told us that it is normal to have to re-intubate more than once, but it is still a little disheartening. We do thank God for vigilant doctors, but we are also sad for Christian. Please continue to keep Christian in your prayers. We are asking God for complete healing of Christian's heart and body. Hold up the rest of our family in prayers, as well. Brenton and Jordan are getting a little tired of the schedule we have been keeping the last couple of weeks and have expressed their displeasure in their own unique ways. Also, Margaret is still recovering from the delivery.

We are encouraged that there is nothing we are going through that Christ has not already gone through and overcome. Speaking of the coming Messiah, Jesus Christ, Isaiah wrote:

> He was despised and rejected by men, a man of sorrows, and familiar with suffering. Like one from whom men hide their faces he was despised, and we esteemed him not.

> Surely he took up our infirmities and carried our sorrows, yet we considered him stricken by God, smitten by him, and afflicted. (Isa. 53:3–4, NIV)

We lean on Christ's experience and on His presence during this time.
God bless.
DCE

Wednesday, May 14, 2003, 9:55 PM

This is going to be short because I am exhausted. Margaret and I did not get much sleep last night because she was not feeling well, so we are turning in early.

Margaret spent much of the day at the hospital with Christian, along with our friend Andrea. Today Christian had his stitches removed and was a lot more alert. He has lost a lot of weight. He is down to a little over 8 pounds. Pray that he will get stronger from the milk and the moving around. And also pray that Margaret and I will get the rest we need.

God bless you.
DCE

Thursday, May 15, 2003, 11:54 PM

Friends,

I want to thank so many of you who have reached out to show your love in word and in deed. It is a blessing to see how God is using you to minister to my family when we need it most. We thank God constantly for His faithfulness shown through your acts. Again, I apologize if I have not returned your messages or taken you up on offers to assist us. It has been a little overwhelming to balance all of the things going on in our lives right now, but please know that we are being taken care of and we may yet call on you for assistance. In the meantime, we appreciate your words of encouragement, your acts of support, and most importantly, your prayers to God for healing on behalf of Christian.

Today, I got to spend a few hours with Christian. He was more alert today and it was wonderful to see his eyes, talk to him, change a diaper, lift him so his bedding could be changed, and let him know that his daddy was near. Before I left to go home, I once again prayed for God's protection, His comfort through the Holy Spirit, and complete healing for Christian's body. Please continue to keep these things in your prayers, as well.

The doctors changed Christian's pain medication yesterday. He is now getting periodic doses of morphine, rather than constant doses of fentanyl and Versed. The idea is to wean him off the pain medications he has been using since his surgery, over two weeks ago. However, he is going through withdrawals in the process since the drugs are narcotic. This is painful for him but part of the healing process. Please pray that Christian would be comforted and protected from affliction.

For Christian to be taken off the respirator and extubated, he needs to get stronger. They have increased his calorie intake and he is receiving respiratory therapy, but he is still weak, tired, and to me, appears frail. Ask God to strengthen Christian's little body and prepare him to breathe on his own.

> Consider it pure joy, my brothers, whenever you face trials of many kinds, because you know that the testing of your faith develops perseverance. Perseverance must finish its work so that you may be mature and complete, not lacking anything. (James 1:2–4, NIV)

Pray that we will expect good from God, that we will stay on this course to maturity and that we may not be lacking in anything.

God bless you and keep you in peace.

Persevering,

DCE

Saturday, May 17, 2003, 12:40 AM

> The LORD is my rock and my fortress and my deliverer; My God, my strength, in whom I will trust; My shield and the horn of my salvation, my stronghold. (Psalm 18:2, KJV)

Today has been sort of a rough day for Christian. When Margaret and I arrived at the hospital, the nurses were preparing to transport him to the catheter lab. They hoped to accomplish two things. First, the doctors wanted to insert a new line into his heart called a PIC line. It would replace the RA line inserted through his chest into his right atrium. The PIC line is an intravenous catheter this is inserted into the vein in his right leg and threaded up to the larger veins in the chest. It is less prone to infection or clotting than the RA line.

Second, the doctors wanted to make sure that Christian's diaphragm was dropping as his lungs filled. It happens occasionally that after heart surgery, the diaphragm does not work properly and give the lungs enough room to expand. It takes minor surgery to correct this. Thankfully, his diaphragm works fine, but while they were investigating, the doctors discovered an area of fluid outside the lungs above the diaphragm that was not allowing the lungs to completely inflate. They drained off some of the fluid and inserted a new drain line to see if any more fluid is produced. This may account for Christian's two failed extubations.

To cap off the early afternoon, Christian received some more blood to keep his blood count high and they removed his RA line. All in all, it was a very exhausting day for the little guy. Despite this, he was pretty alert and Margaret, and I got to spend some time talking to him and entertaining him (Margaret and I have been working on this little vaudeville act that we tried out on him. He was gracious and declined to comment on the routine, but I digress).

Praise God for the doctor's investigation and discovery of the fluid in Christian's chest. Praise God that Christian's RA line was removed before it could get infected or clotted. Praise God that Christian continues to show improvement in his recovery.

Please keep Margaret in your prayers. She is still recovering from the birth and experiencing a lot of pain. Ask God to heal her and give her strength.

The boys are doing a little better this week. They got to spend a lot of time at home with Mom and Dad. Pray that God will comfort them and give them peace while they wait for their brother to come home.

Thank you, all, for your love and your prayer. You are a blessing to our family.

Looking to God for strength,

DCE

Sunday, May 18, 2003, 12:58 AM

All,

Today was family day. In the morning, we celebrated birthdays for my nephew and mom at my parent's house. In the afternoon, Margaret, Brenton, Jordan, and I headed up to the hospital to visit Christian. Because he is more stable, he was moved to another room and the report on him was pretty good. He isn't draining any significant amount of fluid from his chest, his O2 and CO2 levels in his blood are good even when the respirator is hardly helping, and he continues to digest his food.

The big blessing of the day was that the nurse and respiratory therapist were willing to rearrange Christian's equipment so that Margaret could hold him. She got to hold him for nearly an hour while we took pictures of them with Brenton and with Jordan. Margaret was very happy to finally hold her new baby.

Praise God for His mercy and blessing on our family!

DCE

Monday, May 19, 2003, 12:32 AM

> For you created my inmost being; you knit me together in my mother's womb. I praise you because I am fearfully and wonderfully made; your works are wonderful, I know that full well. (Psalm 139:13–14, NIV)

Christian had a good day today. He continues to improve and may get to be extubated this week. Please ask God to strengthen Christian so that he can breathe on his own.

Take a look at our website to see the gift God has given to our family. His works are truly wonderful!

God bless you.

David

♡❋ Margaret's Journal ❋♡

May 19, 2003

Dear Lord,

It has been many days since I wrote Christian's birth story. He will be four weeks old on Thursday. It breaks my heart that he has had so much suffering and complications with his heart and now with his lungs. Before he was born, there were absolutely no signs of problems with his heart from the ultrasound.

I still cry tears every time I think about being separated from him. It is the most emotional pain I have ever experienced in my life. Every morning, I wake up and think that it could not be true. My baby must be alright. This pain is like an ocean that I am being tossed around and around. The song by Jars of Clay called "The Valley" rings over and over in my mind.

Lord, we prayed after our two miscarriages (baby April and Autumn)—we prayed night after night on our knees that You would give us another child. We prayed for months and then we conceived a baby last summer. Lord, You were so faithful the whole pregnancy. You helped me day by day—the trial of David going to the hospital in an ambulance and his emergency surgery—it was frightening. He looked very close to death some days. I praise God that You healed his infection with Your power and Your healing hand. Lord, I know that You can do a mighty work in Christian's life. I know that you have the power to heal.

David has been writing to friends and family every night. We pray that You would be glorified through Christian's life. We pray that You would bring him comfort and healing and peace. Protect his body, mind, and soul from the evil one. We pray that Your will would be done. You know our desires, Lord. Lord, be with us and the boys during this difficult and emotional time.

Lord, I can't wait to hold Christian again. I can't wait to change his diaper, to rock him, to sing to him all day, to hear his cry and answer it, to see his smile, to hear his laugh, to nurse him, to burp him, to bottle feed if necessary, to bathe him, to take him outdoors in the stroller on a walk or to the park, to show him the ocean, the moon, sun, stars—your beautiful creations, to see his beautiful eyes every day, and to kiss him every day on the cheeks. Oh Lord, You know these are just a few of the things I look forward to. There are many more. Be with Christian every moment of today because I can't. He is Yours. Help me to understand your plan.

CHAPTER 4
Setback

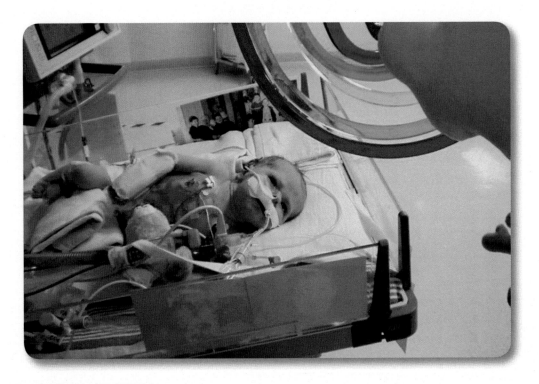

Tuesday, May 20, 2003, 12:15 AM

Friends,

Today was one of those roller-coaster days. As always, it is sometimes difficult to see the big picture when we are so close to the subject. It is discouraging and emotionally draining when we don't see the progress we hope for. Please pray that God would give us peace and courage at this time.

Christian's stomach has not been responding well to the milk/formula and this morning, there was blood in his stool. They have taken him off of his feeds, taken a bunch of x-rays, and have put him on IV nutrition and antibiotics. The concern is that his intestines are not receiving enough blood or oxygen and could get an infection. Please pray that the doctors would accurately diagnose the problem and properly treat it.

When I last checked, he is sleeping much of the time, but we are concerned that he is not building up enough strength to be taken off the respirator. Ask God to strengthen Christian's body so that he can breathe on his own.

Thank you for your prayers. Thank you for your support. You are a blessing.

Riding the roller coaster,

DCE

Tuesday, May 20, 2003, 10:59 PM

There are a few *hospital* words that are good to hear. My dad is quite fond of *stable*. As for me, I like *recovering* and *extubate*. Some words are not nice to hear. Today, the word was *setback*. This is not the word Margaret or I wanted to hear, but that is the word the doctor used. As I mentioned in my last email, Christian had some blood in his stool and the doctors had already begun to take some preventative steps. The surgeon suspects that Christian might have necrotic ischemic colitis. In simple terms, this means that the heart is not sending enough blood, and oxygen to allow the colon to do its job of digesting food. The thinking is that perhaps they were rushing a little to start Christian on higher calories and at the same time, reducing the assistance from the respirator. The doctors are watching him very carefully to make sure he does not present any signs of infection. They anticipate that Christian will need seven to ten days of rest for him to heal before they can start feeding him milk again and before they can extubate him.

Margaret and I both spent time with Christian today. It was good to see his eyes and touch him. He is getting pretty long and may not fit in his bed much longer. Despite the scars and IVs, he is a beautiful baby.

In addition to the emotional drain, Margaret and I are feeling the physical effects. Margaret's back and neck are beginning to bother her. This is mostly due to the condition of Highway 101, our route to and from the hospital each day. Also, I had sinus problems all day, so I did not spend as much time as I wanted with Christian.

Please pray that Christian will get the rest he needs to heal from these intestinal problems. Pray that his body will be strong and will recover from all that has been done to his body. Ask God to strengthen Margaret and me as we struggle to meet the needs of Brenton and Jordan while attending to Christian. Ask God to grant us rest, peace, and grace.

Today, the Holy Spirit led me to the fortieth Psalm. It talks about how God provides for us and how we can trust Him. It starts, however, with our responsibility. The author, David, says, "I waited patiently for the Lord; and He inclined to me, and heard my cry." The phrase "waited patiently" could also be translated "waited intently." This implies action. We wait for the Lord, expecting Him to do something. When I cry out, He hears me. When I trust, He shows Himself trustworthy. When I am afflicted or needy, He is my help and my deliverer. In our situation, Margaret and I have no choice but to wait—wait for Christian to recover, wait for Christian's heart to be repaired, wait for life at home to be more *normal*. We do, however, have a choice as to how we wait. We could wait idly and accomplish nothing but warm a chair in the hospital. We could wait impatiently, making the hospital staff anxious and wearing ourselves out. Or we could wait intently and expect that God will put before us opportunities to honor and glorify Him. Being an immediate-gratification-kind of guy, it is difficult for me to wait. But I will. And I will do it patiently because I am waiting for the Lord.

Thank you for your notes of encouragement and for your support in prayer. Know that God is honoring those prayers.

God bless you.

Waiting,

DCE

 Margaret's Journal

May 22, 2003

Dear Lord,

Today, we went to see Christian together. We took the boys to Dana and Mike's at ten this morning. Then, they went with Julie to karate class and the park. Now, we need to pick up the kids at Julie's house. She has been such a blessing to us. The boys have such a good time at their house. Bless her family as she is waiting for Graham to return from the war in Iraq. He is still there. Now it looks like he will not return home until November. It has been since February when he left with the Army National Guard. God, we pray that you would reunite their family soon.

I look forward to the day when you reunite our family of five. We have never had all three boys in the same room or all five of us in the same room yet. Wow. Lord, bring us unity.

We continue to pray for healing for Christian. We pray his lungs would remain clear and his heart would beat at a good rate and that he would have good blood gas levels. Lord, we pray for continued healing of his intestines.

Thursday, May 22, 2003, 12:03 AM

> Is any one of you in trouble? He should pray. Is anyone happy? Let him sing songs of praise. Is any one of you sick? He should call the elders of the church to pray over him and anoint him with oil in the name of the Lord. And the prayer offered in faith will make the sick person well; the Lord will raise him up. If he has sinned, he will be forgiven. (James 5:13–15, NIV)

Margaret and I spent much of the day with Christian. The nurses were fairly positive and the staff thinks that Christian is probably on the mend from the colitis. This was good news to hear and made our time with Christian a little less stressful. Pray that Christian would continue to heal from the colitis.

We had asked two of our pastors, Jim and Paul, to come to the hospital to pray for Christian today. After lunch, the four of us prayed over Christian and Jim anointed him with oil. We are thankful for the ministry of Jim and Paul and were blessed by the time they spent with us.

I would like to ask you to pray for some of the other patients we have come in contact with. There are three other children in the same room as Christian: two are recovering from heart surgery and another is very ill. Pray that God would bring healing and would continue to give us opportunities to minister to their families. At the hospital, we also ran into an old friend, Bill, who we haven't seen for a few years. His five-day-old daughter had a seizure and is in the NICU. Pray that God would heal Bill's daughter and that He would comfort Bill and his wife.

Thank you again for all of your encouragement. Your emails, phone calls, and cards are much appreciated as we go through this unpredictable journey. God bless you.

Continuing to pray in faith,

DCE

Thursday, May 22, 2003, 11:57 PM

Christian is continuing to heal from his colitis. He is getting lots of rest and is gaining strength. His grandparents (Margaret's mom and dad) and his great aunt and uncle got to visit him today while he was awake. It was very exciting for him.

Today, Christian is four weeks old. While the hospital is not where we expected to be at this time, we are thankful that we have had these four weeks to spend with him.

We thank God for this wonderful gift of a son.

We thank God for nurses who are so alert and attentive to Christian.

We thank God for so many people who have taken care of our physical and emotional needs.

We thank God for His loving care for Christian, Jordan, Brenton, Margaret, and me.

> The LORD is high above all nations, and his glory above the heavens. Who is like unto the LORD our God, who dwelleth on high, Who humbleth himself to behold the things that are in heaven, and in the earth! (Psalm 113:4–6, KJV)

God bless you.

DCE

Saturday, May 24, 2003, 12:01 AM

Yes, it's late again, so I will make this short. Christian continues to heal. The doctors are pleased with his progress. They have already started to *sprint* him (lowering the amount of assistance given by the respirator) during the day. The big blessing of the day is that I got to hold Christian in my arms for about an hour. This is the first time I have held him since the day he was born. For the last twenty or so minutes, he had his eyes open. Hopefully, he will have a better idea of who daddy is now.

I went in to work today to discuss my schedule with my manager. It was good to see my coworkers and receive their concerns and support personally. I will be starting back to work after Memorial Day. Please pray for Margaret's strength as she will be taking on more without my help. She needs strength and peace as she continues to recover from birth and will be doing a lot more driving to and from the hospital.

We appreciate and covet your prayers. Thank you for your support and care.

God bless you.

DCE

Sunday, May 25, 2003, 11:13 PM

All,

Please pray for our family. Christian is making slow improvements. He is still healing from the colitis but was started on medication to control the amount of blood getting to his lungs—there seems to be too much going to them. We are still waiting for him to take Margaret's milk again and look forward to him being off the respirator, but we have not been given any idea of when this might happen.

Brenton and Jordan had a busy week and got to see their brother today. Christian even opened his eyes while his big brothers were visiting. It was good for the older boys to interact with Christian. However, Brenton and Jordan have been getting on each other's nerves lately.

Margaret and I are worn out. The marathon is making us tired.

Please pray for Christian's complete healing and that he would be able to come home soon. Pray for God's peace with Brenton and Jordan. Ask God to give Margaret and me wisdom to manage our time and an extra measure of His strength.

> Give ear to my words, O LORD, consider my sighing. Listen to my cry for help, my King and my God, for to you I pray. In the morning, O LORD, you hear my voice; in the morning I lay my requests before you and wait in expectation. (Psalm 5:1–3, NIV)

Thank you for your support and prayer.

God bless.

DCE

Monday, May 26, 2003, 9:59 PM

Today was another emotionally difficult day for us and a physically difficult one for Christian. At 9:00 AM, Christian was finding the respiration tube very annoying and was fighting with it. Rather than just try to secure it to him, the doctors decided that it might be a good time to see how well he might do off of the respirator. They extubated him and got him to calm down a little. We got in at about 11:00 AM and we found him wide awake and quite active. Brenton and Jordan each got to spend a little time with Christian while he was awake and we got some pictures. However, a little after noon, the blood tests showed that he was not getting rid of his CO2 the way he should, and by 1:00 PM, he was beginning to turn blue. They intubated him again and put him back on the respirator.

Christian managed to stay off the respirator for about four hours this time. This is much better than the first time he was extubated when he only lasted about thirty minutes, and the second time, when he went for nearly ninety minutes without assistance. While we are thankful that he was able to go longer without the respirator this time, we are very concerned that he is still not strong enough to stay off it.

With Christian still on the respirator, it is very difficult for Margaret and me to see any end to this race. We are not sure how to plan or what to hope or what to expect. Each time we hit this dip in the roller coaster, we try to protect ourselves by not getting our expectations too high. At the same time, we pray and hope that Christian will recover and don't understand why the progress seems so slow.

We know that all of this is just part of a larger plan that God has for each of us. However, we feel like we are trying to see that plan while peering through a straw—there is so much happening, but we see so little and are concerned only with what we see. It can be so consuming that we just want to run away.

> My heart is in anguish within me, and the terrors of death have fallen upon me. Fear and trembling come upon me; And horror has overwhelmed me. And I said, "Oh, that I had wings like a dove! I would fly away and be at rest. Behold, I would wander far away, I would lodge in the wilderness. I would hasten to my place of refuge from the stormy wind and tempest." (Psalm 55:4–8)

Please pray that God will give Christian strength in his body. Pray that God's very breath would fill Christian's lungs with life and allow him to be free of the respirator. Ask that God would give us a glimpse of hope for Christian's recovery.

As always, we remain obedient to God's will, learning to trust that He is in control, and resting in the presence of His Son.

God's blessings on you all,
DCE

Tuesday, May 27, 2003, 11:57 PM

It has been a long day.

Today was my first day back at work (to actually do some work) in over four weeks. Between the calls from the doctors and then calls to the family, I'm not sure I really earned my pay today. At ten this morning, I had to give consent for Christian to be taken in for a catheter procedure. They wanted to measure the pressure in his heart chambers and lungs and if necessary, insert a shunt. The idea was to investigate why Christian failed his last extubation. He went into the procedure just a little after eleven o'clock and was expected to be out in a few hours.

I picked up Margaret in the afternoon and went to the hospital expecting to see Christian sedated and resting after the procedure. Instead, we walked in as two nurses and one respiratory therapist worked rather urgently on Christian. At that time, we weren't sure what they were doing and we didn't want to bother them until things were a little less hectic. While all this was happening, one of the surgeons informed us that Christian would probably be having his next surgery, the Glenn, either this week or next. This was a little shocking as we did not expect Christian to have this surgery for at least another month or so. She told us that Christian's surgeon would be speaking with us today to give us the details. As the x-ray machine was brought in to take pictures of Christian, our heads were spinning with information and the immediate concern for Christian's condition. In the midst of the activity, I was able to reach over, touch Christian's head, and whisper a prayer of protection and grace for him. The stress was getting a bit high, so we left the room and went to the chapel to pray. Again, we committed Christian, his care, and his healing to the grace of God.

When we returned to Christian's room, things were a bit more settled. The nurse told us that after Christian returned from the procedure, his oxygen saturation dropped, his heart rate rose, and his lungs were filling with fluid. They think it might have been a reaction to the dye used in the catheter procedure.

The cardiologist, Dr. Perry, spoke with us and explained the findings of the procedure. It seems that the heart, as it is currently configured, is pumping too much blood to the lungs and not quite enough to the rest of the body. This could explain why he was unable to get rid of the CO_2 gas as he should and why he might have ended up with colitis. After that, we spoke with the surgeon, Dr. Reddy. He explained that to get Christian off the respirator, the amount of blood going to the lungs had to be lowered. This could be done in one of two ways. The first method would be to *band* the artery from the heart to the lungs, restricting the flow of blood. The second method would be to perform the Glenn surgery early. This surgery would arrange Christian's cardio-pulmonary system so that the heart would pump blood only to the body and the blood from the upper part of the body (head and arms) would go through the lungs and then return to the heart.

Each surgery has its pros and cons. Dr. Reddy has already put us on the surgery schedule for Monday, but it is up to us to make the decision. We will need to decide which surgery we want Christian to have and the day we want him to have it. Since this would be his second major surgery in six weeks (plus three invasive catheter procedures), we are a little concerned about the timing. We are also disappointed that any surgery will delay the opportunity to bring him home. Please pray that God would give us wisdom for this decision and continued strength for this marathon. Also, pray for Dr. Reddy, as he would be the surgeon to perform the operation.

Join me and praise God that Brenton and Jordan got to see their little brother while he was awake and without a tube in his mouth.

Praise God for Dr. Perry and his expertise.

Praise God for Olga, Christian's nurse today, for her hard work and attentiveness.

Praise God for Dr. Reddy.

Praise God for each day we get to spend with Christian.

Praise God for His faithfulness even when our faith falters.

> Be gracious to me, O God, be gracious to me, for my soul takes refuge in Thee; and in the shadow of Thy wings I will take refuge, until destruction passes by. (Psalm 57:1)

Thank you all for your continued prayer and support. God has blessed us with you.

In Christ,

DCE

CHAPTER 5

Second Surgery

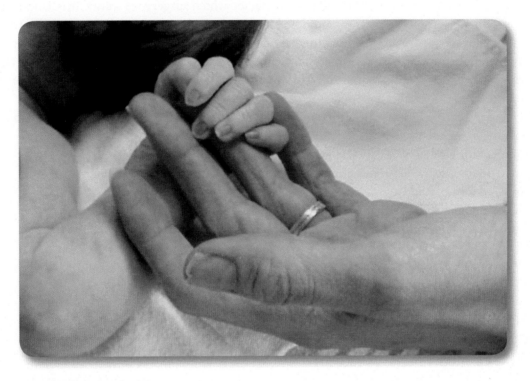

Thursday, May 29, 2003, 7:36 AM

All,

I want to thank so many of you for your words of encouragement. God has used you to shore up our faith and to walk next to us on this road.

Christian was doing pretty well today. Margaret and I went to the hospital this afternoon to be with him, and he was alert and active. The latest news we received was that the surgery would probably be on Tuesday. This is already an answer to prayer! Regardless of the surgery he might have, an extra day to get strong and get rest is a good thing. Please continue to pray that God would keep Christian healthy, well-rested, and strong. Also, pray that God would grant Margaret and me wisdom as we still have not decided which surgery Christian should have next week.

A couple of people at our church have suggested a day to fast and pray for Christian. For those of you unfamiliar with fasting, it is a spiritual discipline that allows you to focus your prayer without the distractions of feeding your body. The suggestion was that those who are interested would refrain from food from sunup to sundown on Friday, May 30, committing that time to pray for God's grace and healing on behalf of Christian. If this is something you would be interested in doing, I would like to recommend that you visit http://www. spirithome.com/spirdisc.html for a description of the discipline of fasting and how the practice is described in the Bible. This would be both a fast for God's grace and a fast of preparation as Christian is about to have surgery again. Jesus's sermon in the sixth chapter of Matthew describes this spiritual discipline as something between you and God the Father, so please do not feel that you have to communicate your desire or decision to fast with me or anyone else. It is simply an appropriate occasion to consider this discipline.

May God give you the peace that can only be found in His Son, Jesus Christ through the Holy Spirit. See Philippians 2:1–2.

DCE

Friday, May 30, 2003, 12:36 AM

Good evening all,

Today has been a relatively peaceful day for Christian. He spent most of the day resting, but when I visited in the afternoon, he was awake and following me with his eyes. He is fairly comfortable. The nurses did not have to give him any extra sedation or pain medicine. We listened to some music together and I talked to him.

It is difficult for us to fathom that Christian will have another surgery in just a few days. We were hopeful that we would be able to bring Christian home before he had another surgery. Seeing him still intubated, unable to take any milk, and just healing from his last surgery makes considering further recovery in the hospital challenging. Please keep us in your prayers.

DCE

Saturday, May 31, 2003, 12:14 AM

Never be lacking in zeal, but keep your spiritual fervor, serving the Lord. Be joyful in hope, patient in affliction, faithful in prayer. Share with God's people who are in need. Practice hospitality. (Rom. 12:11–13, NIV)

It is a privilege to interact regularly with people who serve the Lord with passion, who are joyful, patient, faithful, and who share from their resources. Your prayers and acts of service are instrumental in giving us hope each time we enter the hospital, peace each night as we go to sleep, and confidence that Jesus is Lord and Jesus is present. Praise God for each of you.

I want to thank those of you who were praying and fasting on our behalf. We were tasked with deciding what kind of surgery Christian should have next. Having never been in this situation before, we knew we needed Godly wisdom to make this decision. God made sure that all of our questions were answered so that we could be informed about this aspect of Christian's care. Today, we told the surgeon that we wanted to proceed with the Glenn surgery, which would provide a more permanent solution for Christian's current inability to be off the respirator. The surgery is now scheduled for Tuesday morning, June 3.

Margaret, Brenton, Jordan, and I got to spend some time with Christian. He was awake much of the time, so the three boys got to interact a little. As an added blessing, Margaret and I got to hold Christian for an hour each. He seemed quite comfortable, as he fell asleep each time we held him. This connection made me feel more confident about the decision we had made about his next surgery.

Please continue to keep Christian in your prayers. He needs to get rest and remain healthy in preparation for his surgery. Being in a hospital can often expose a patient to infections or other ailments. The doctors and nurses are doing all they can to keep Christian comfortable, rested, and free from anything that could keep him from surgery. Ask that God would give them wisdom and insight to accomplish this goal.

Please lay at the feet of our Creator, the desire to see Christian fully healed and restored. As always, we submit to His will as we make our requests known to Him in the name of His Son, Jesus Christ.

Thankfully,

DCE

Monday, June 2, 2003, 12:02 AM

All,

It has been a peaceful weekend for Christian and for the rest of the family. Christian has been getting a lot of rest, has remained healthy, and seems to be growing much stronger. Likewise, Margaret and I feel rested and stronger as we anticipate Christian's surgery this week. We praise God for keeping Christian in His hands and for showing such grace to our family!

Yesterday, Brenton and Jordan were able to visit their brother and entertain him. They spent a little time holding Christian's hand and talking with him. Today, Christian was visited by a set of grandparents, a close friend, and one of our pastors. Christian keeps a very full social schedule for someone only five weeks old.

I want to thank all of you who have prayed for Christian, specifically regarding his upcoming surgery. So far, the surgery is still scheduled for Tuesday morning. I hope to have more details on Monday. We continue to ask God to grant the surgeons wisdom as they assess Christian's condition and skill as they operate on him. We are also asking God for healing mercies during his recovery as this is another open-heart surgery.

We continue to praise God for you. Your generosity and willingness to hold our family in prayer have been a great blessing to us. May God bless you and keep you in peace.

In peace,
DCE

Monday, June 2, 2003, 6:57 PM

All,

Just a quick update, Christian will be going into surgery at 7:00 AM tomorrow morning (6/3). The surgery is expected to take five to six hours. Please continue to keep him in your prayers—that he would be protected from anything that might keep him from being healed. I will be staying at the hospital overnight so that I can see him in for surgery. Margaret will be home trying to get some much-needed rest.

God bless you and thank you!
DCE

Tuesday, June 3, 2003, 10:07 PM

Many are the plans in a man's heart, but it is the Lord's purpose that prevails. (Prov. 19:21, NIV)

As some of you know, Christian's surgery was postponed today. At 4:00 AM, he started to develop an arrhythmia (his heart suddenly beats at a faster rate and then returns to a normal rate). Much of the morning was spent trying to control this as the surgeon does not want this to happen during surgery. We thought Christian might get surgery in the afternoon, but after consulting with a specialist, it was decided to postpone surgery until at least Thursday. He is on the schedule for Thursday morning, but it is dependent on how well his heart performs. In spite of the arrhythmia, all of Christian's other vital signs were excellent. Praise God!

While it is disappointing to have this delay, this is an answer to prayer. We asked God to keep away anything that would keep Christian from healing—surgery with an arrhythmia would have been one of those things. Furthermore, we are always praying that God would grant our doctors and nurses wisdom and we believe they made wise decisions today.

Margaret and I did not get much rest last night so please ask God to give us peace and rest this evening. Also, pray that God would bring peace to Christian's heart and body so that he can prepare for his surgery.

Thank you for your help, understanding, prayer, and care. You are an encouragement to us.

God bless you.
DCE

Wednesday, June 4, 2003, 11:04 PM

All,

Thank you for your continued support in prayer and care. We have received so much from so many of you—encouraging words, meals, care for Brenton and Jordan, and your very presence. We are grateful.

We spoke with the surgeons today and were told that Christian was on the schedule to have surgery on Thursday afternoon, probably around 1:00 PM. From what we understand, this will be Dr. Reddy's only surgery for the day. In the meantime, Christian had a very good day. He did not have any further arrhythmia and was awake and alert for a few hours. Margaret and I spent some time entertaining him and talking to him, which was fun.

Please commit Christian to God's hands, particularly for this surgery. We are asking God to mend Christian's heart and to bring about a complete and easy recovery. We lay these requests at His feet, knowing that He is in control, that He loves Christian, and that He knows what is best for him.

> May your unfailing love rest upon us, O Lord, even as we put our hope in You. (Psalm 33:22, NIV)

God bless.
DCE

Thursday, June 5, 2003, 9:01 PM

All,

Well, we continue to wait for Christian's surgery. We had hoped to see Christian go in for his surgery this afternoon but were informed late in the morning that he would probably not get in today. Instead, they have scheduled him for tomorrow (Friday) morning as the first one for the morning. We continue to ask for God's blessing on Christian and on the men and women who will be caring for him in the operating room. Thank you for joining us in this prayer.

God bless you all,
David

Friday, June 6, 2003, 7:44 AM

All,

Christian was taken to surgery this morning at 6:50 AM. Praise God that Christian had a good rest and some extra days before he went in. Praise God that we got to spend some extra time with him this week without a bunch of tubes going in and out of him.

Ask that God would extend his healing hands to Christian through His Son, Jesus Christ, the great Physician. Request that God would send His Holy Spirit to be a Presence in that operating room today, that there would be peace, comfort, and order. Thank you for keeping Him in your prayers.

> Give ear, O Lord, to my prayer; and give heed to the voice of my supplication! In the day of my trouble
> I shall call upon Thee, for Thou wilt answer me. (Psalm 86:6–7)

God bless and keep you.
DCE

Friday, June 6, 2003, 5:14 PM

All,

Christian came out of surgery at approximately 1:00 PM this afternoon. Dr. Reddy, the surgeon, was very positive about the outcome and anticipates that Christian may be off the respirator after a few days. Our hope is that he will recover quickly and be able to breathe on his own. He looks a little worn out and is a little *puffy*, but his vital signs seem to be strong.

Margaret and I want to thank you for keeping Christian in your prayers and for being such an encouragement to us. This has been a very trying week for us, but the stress has been lessened by your support.

DCE

Psalm 95

CHAPTER 6
Recovery, Again

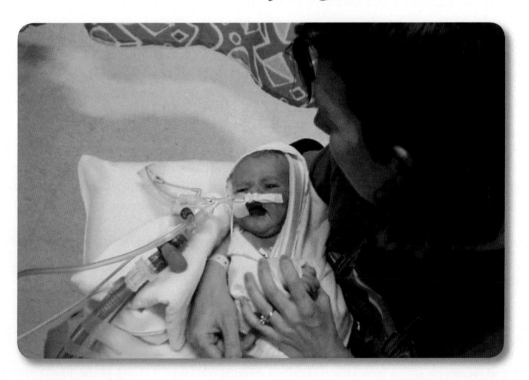

Sunday, June 8, 2003, 3:33 PM

Then the King [Jesus] will say to those on his right, "Come, you who are blessed by my Father; take your inheritance, the kingdom prepared for you since the creation of the world. For I was hungry and you gave me something to eat, I was thirsty and you gave me something to drink, I was a stranger and you invited me in, I needed clothes and you clothed me, I was sick and you looked after me, I was in prison and you came to visit me."

Then the righteous will answer him, "Lord, when did we see you hungry and feed you, or thirsty and give you something to drink? When did we see you a stranger and invite you in, or needing clothes and clothe you? When did we see you sick or in prison and go to visit you?"

The King will reply, "I tell you the truth, whatever you did for one of the least of these brothers of mine, you did for me." (Matt. 25:34–40, NIV)

Margaret and I are so blessed to be the recipients of your care and support. From providing meals to doing our yard work, to spending time with us at the hospital, to being steadfast in your prayer for us, you have been faithful to Christ's call to care for the *least of these*. Thank you for your love and hard work. We praise God for the people He has brought into our lives to draw us close to Him.

As you may have guessed, last week was very difficult for the family. Christian's surgery kept getting postponed, Margaret was battling her allergies, and we are physically and emotionally worn out from the roller coaster. Despite this, we have much to praise God for:

- Christian's surgery went well and he is recovering.
- Margaret and I were able to spend a lot of time with Christian.
- We were able to get some family pictures of all five of us.
- Brenton and Jordan had lots to do this week with grandparents and friends.
- We have had opportunities to minister to others at the hospital as we have been getting to know other parents.

Margaret and a friend went to the hospital today to visit Christian (I am home with a cold). Christian continues to recover and he is being watched very closely. Please pray that he did not catch anything from me and that the doctors and nurses would show wisdom and care as they adjust his medications and breathing support. Continue to pray for Christian's complete healing.

There is another patient in Christian's room. Her name is Cara and she is nineteen. She had her fifth surgery on Thursday and it was very difficult (her surgery is why Christian's surgery was postponed). I had an opportunity to have breakfast with her father on Saturday morning and he and his wife have demonstrated a strong faith in God during Cara's nineteen years of life. She has gone through a lot but is a blessing to her family and to her friends. Ask God to comfort and heal her.

Thank you for your prayer. Thank you for your encouragement. Thank you for your care. God bless you and keep you.

In His care,
DCE

Monday, June 9, 2003, 10:57 PM

> But as for me, my prayer is to Thee, O Lord, at an acceptable time; O God, in the greatness of Thy loving kindness, answer me with Thy saving truth. Deliver me from the mire, and do not let me sink; May I be delivered from my foes, and from the deep waters. May the flood of water not overflow me, and may the deep not swallow me up, And may the pit not shut its mouth on me. (Psalm 69:13–15)

Dear friends and family,

The day started out a little rough for Margaret and me as we are both feeling the strain of this trial. We are struggling emotionally and physically and are questioning God's plan for us at this time. We are praying that God would give us strength and grace to face what He has chosen not to reveal to us.

Margaret was able to spend some time with Christian this afternoon and early evening. He continues to be stable as he is slowly weaned off of medication and assistance. The biggest concern is for infections that are common after surgery. With so many tubes and lines going in and out of his body, the chance for infection is increased. We are told that he will be given much time to rest tonight without too much fussing over him or attempts to make changes to his medications or respirator. Pray that God would grant Christian comfort and rest tonight and that He would protect him from any infection or other hindrances to his recovery.

We continue to be blessed by your prayers, concern, help, and love. So many of you are a testimony to God's providence in our lives.

With much gratitude,
DCE

Tuesday, June 10, 2003, 11:35 PM

All,

Thank you for your prayer and for your care. We see the evidence of God answering the requests made on our behalf. Christian had a very peaceful day. I spent some time this afternoon and evening with him and he is looking much better. He is not requiring as much medication as before and he had another line removed (chest tube). He started taking breast milk last night through his NG tube and has been tolerating it well. These are all good indications of recovery.

We have been told that the doctors will attempt to extubate him tomorrow. They are eager to get him off the respirator before any damage is done to his lungs from being on it so long. Please pray that this would be successful and that Christian would be able to breathe on his own. Another concern is that Christian has pneumonia in one of his lungs. They suspected this a couple of days ago and began treating it then. The doctors are confident that they were able to address this early enough to prevent any real problems. Please pray that the treatment is successful and that he would be healed from this virus.

Lately, I have tended to be focused on the needs of my own family, perhaps to the exclusion of others who are hurting. Today, I received news of three families that are in need of healing right now. Please pray for Ken who is recovering from an unexpected colon surgery. Pray for John who will need to undergo further chemotherapy. Pray for God's peace and comfort on Staci and Jeff who lost their child today. As you go through your day tomorrow, commit them to the Lord's care by name.

> Now we who are strong ought to bear the weaknesses of those without strength and not just please ourselves. (Rom. 15:1)

In His care,
DCE

Thursday, June 12, 2003, 12:21 AM

> How blessed is he who considers the helpless; The Lord will deliver him in a day of trouble. The Lord will protect him, and keep him alive, And he shall be called blessed upon the earth; And do not give him over to the desire of his enemies. The Lord will sustain him upon his sickbed; In his illness, Thou does restore him to health. (Ps. 41:1–3)

All,

Thank you for committing Christian's health and healing to the Lord. Your care and concern will be blessed.

Christian continues to make small improvements. While the doctors decided not to extubate Christian today, he is not requiring very much assistance from the respirator. They are still concerned with the complications that can occur from being on a respirator too long, and with the pneumonia he is currently being treated for. We continue to ask God for His healing mercies on Christian.

I had a couple of wonderful blessings today as I was able to talk to two good friends today. These two men have been a source of encouragement to me for many years and it was good to talk about how God is working in their lives and to receive support from them. I am grateful to God for these guys.

I would also like to ask that you keep a ten-year-old boy named Peter in your prayers. He is going through chemotherapy right now.

God's blessings on you all,
DCE

Friday, June 13, 2003, 10:43 PM

> Bless the Lord, O my soul; And all that is within me, bless His holy name. Bless the Lord, O my soul, And forget none of His benefits; Who pardons all your iniquities; Who heals all your diseases; Who redeems your life from the pit; Who crowns you with loving kindness and compassion. (Psalm 103:1–4)

Each time you pray for our family, give us a hug, bring us a meal, cry with us, or show us how much you love us, you remind us of the Lord's benefits—His healing, His forgiveness, His redemption, His mercy, and His compassion. Thank you for the reminder.

For the last couple of days, Christian has been building up strength while battling various infections. We are still waiting to hear from the doctors about Christian's progress with pneumonia, and we were pleased to hear that his last blood culture came up negative for a yeast infection. During the day, the doctors have decreased the amount of breathing assistance the respirator gives to Christian. This *sprinting* is designed to prepare him to be off the respirator. During the night, the assistance is increased slightly to give him a rest. To strengthen him, he has been taking breast milk mixed with a little formula, increasing the calories. He seems to be digesting it well.

While it is difficult for us to see him still on the respirator and fighting bugs, we praise God that Christian is making small improvements. We continue to ask God for Christian's complete healing and the opportunity to bring him home soon. This has been a long trial for us. I realize that others have gone through much worse and much longer ordeals. We thank God for His faithfulness—that he has shown Himself to be a trustworthy and present Father. We know that, even when our faith is weak, He will never abandon us.

God be praised!

In His care,

DCE

Sunday, June 15, 2003, 12:16 AM

> For just as the sufferings of Christ flow over into our lives, so also through Christ our comfort overflows. (2 Cor. 1:5, NIV)

We praise God for the comfort of His Son in the midst of our struggle. When we lack faith, He comforts. When we lose heart, He comforts. When we are tired, He comforts. Praise Him for His mercy.

Christian continues to struggle with various infections and is now on four different antibiotics. Please pray that God would heal these infections and protect Christian from further exposure to viruses and bacteria. Christian is breathing well and we anticipate that he will be extubated next week. Ask God to grant him the strength to breathe on his own.

Please pray for Cara. She is a nineteen-year-old who just had her fifth surgery last week. She has had a very difficult week and is struggling to recover. Pray for strength and comfort for her parents.

God bless you.

DCE

Sunday, June 15, 2003, 11:02 PM

> I have no greater joy than this, to hear of my children walking in the truth. (3 John 1:4)

Our pastor spoke on this passage today, emphasizing the importance of fatherhood. I have to tell you that I love being a father. Despite the difficulties inherent in the role, it has been a joy to watch Brenton, Jordan, and now, Christian develop and grow. I see glimpses of what they will be like as young men, as husbands, as fathers. I pray that when these boys that God has entrusted to me have left home, I will have the honor of hearing how they are walking in the truth. Fathers, may God grant you this honor, as well.

I had the privilege of spending my Father's Day with my family. We spent a few hours with Christian, entertaining him and fussing over him. He was alert and in a good mood today and enjoyed having his brothers over for a visit. We discovered a pacifier that would work while he is still on a breathing tube, so he spent about thirty minutes sucking on that and seemed pretty happy with the new toy. He continues to tolerate the breast milk, which he still received through his NG tube, and he is putting on some weight. We praise God for His blessings of healing and contentment on Christian.

Our big concern right now is the volume of antibiotics that Christian is receiving. It seems that all we have heard this week is that a new *bug* was discovered and that he would be started on yet another medication. We finally had an opportunity to discuss this with one of the surgeons today. He admitted that they were not sure what was going on, but that he could not possibly have that many infections and still be as healthy as he is. They hope to figure out why he is testing positive for these infections by tomorrow or Tuesday and settle on a treatment. Please keep the medical staff in your prayers—they need wisdom and good decision-making as they care for Christian and the other patients.

Speaking of other patients, please continue to keep Cara and her family in your prayers. Cara has made some small progress, but it is a tough battle for her. Ask that God would keep her in His protective and healing care.

Thank you so much for your words of encouragement and your constant support. You continue to be a blessing to me and my family and we daily see the evidence of God's grace in your actions. May God grant you the blessings of peace.

Holding on to Jesus,
DCE

♡❀ Margaret's Journal ❀♡

June 16, 2003

Dear Lord,

I have prayed night and day for Christian since the day he was born. Thank You for listening and I know you hear my prayers.

Thank You that you answered my prayer that we could have a picture together as a family. I prayed we would all be in one room together. It was not easy but You answered our prayer. Thank You again that You also made a way for Christian to have my breast milk again starting June 9. It has been a whole week, and we praise God for that.

Right now, we pray for protection for all of his body and especially his organs. They discovered many infections last week that he is battling. We pray his body will be able to fight the battle of having too much yeast. Lord, I pray that you would give the doctors wisdom in managing all of the antibiotics Christian is on. I pray for the decision to extubate him, and I pray, Lord, that You would give them the cue. Lord, we pray You would continue to clear his lungs so that he may breathe on his own and that You would fill his lungs with Your very breath of life.

"Let every breath praise the Lord."

We look forward to giving You all the glory.

Also, thank You that we found a pacifier that Sweet Pea was able to use while on the breathing tube. Praise God that we were all together on Father's Day even in the same hospital room. Amen.

CHAPTER 7

Off the Respirator

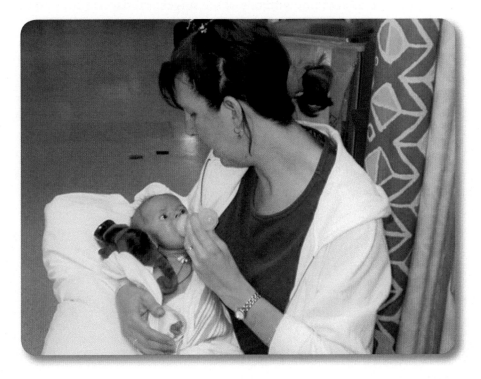

Tuesday, June 17, 2003, 12:41 AM

All,

I would just like to make a quick request:

The doctors are planning to extubate Christian on Tuesday morning (6/17). Please pray that Christian will be strong and healthy for this and that he could stay off the respirator. Thank you and God bless.

DCE

Tuesday, June 17, 2003, 11:36 PM

All,

In case you haven't heard, Christian was extubated today at 12:15 PM. As I write this, he is doing well. He is getting a little oxygen from a cannula (a tube with two little pointy openings that go near the nostrils) and they have him wrapped up in a blanket tonight to help him sleep. Margaret and I got to hold him for hours this afternoon, the first time since his last surgery. Praise God for this blessing. We feel like first-time parents again.

We have a meeting tomorrow with the team of doctors that are caring for Christian. Our hope is to come away with the plan for the rest of Christian's recovery. The extubation is a major milestone, but he still has a couple of lines left in him and he is still fighting three infections. Pray that we will have the wisdom to ask the smart questions and that the doctors will have the wisdom to determine the best course of action for Christian.

> The Lord is my strength and my shield; My heart trusts in him, and I am helped. My heart leaps for joy And I will give thanks to him in song. (Psalm 28:7, NIV)

Please join Margaret, Brenton, Jordan, and me in giving thanks to God, our strength and shield. May He richly bless you.
DCE

Wednesday, June 18, 2003, 11:52 PM

All,

As I write this, Christian is sleeping peacefully and continues to improve. Margaret and I got to hold him quite a bit today. He is a little cranky, probably because he has not had anything to eat since early Tuesday morning. They will start him up on his feeds again tomorrow morning through the NG tube.

We spoke with the doctors today and found out the milestones we need to reach before Christian is released. First, he needs to maintain his airway, which he is currently doing. Second, he needs to be free from infections. He is currently being treated for three different infections and being closely monitored to see if the antibiotics are working. Third, he needs to have all his IV lines out. He currently has two lines. We are committing these milestones to God and relying on His timing and plan.

Now that Christian has been extubated, he will start getting physical therapy to teach him how to suck and swallow (essential if he is to nurse) and to move his head and limbs. Please pray that he will be able to nurse.

Join us in lifting up Cara, the nineteen-year-old heart patient I wrote about previously. Little steps of progress are being made, but they are hard-won. Cara is strong, her parents are hopeful, and God is faithful.

Thank you again for your prayer and support.
DCE

Friday, June 20, 2003, 12:20 AM

All,

Continue to keep Christian in your prayers. He was much more content today since they started feeding him again. However, he was showing signs of infections with a fever, higher heart rate, and an increased white blood cell count. They replaced one of his major IV lines with one new one, and he will have to have a further one put in tomorrow in the catheter lab. Ask God to give him the strength to fight off these infections and to keep him healthy even with the new IV lines.

Thank you all for your prayers, your friendship, and your care.

God bless you.
DCE

Friday, June 20, 2003, 11:54 PM

> And the God of all grace, who called you to His eternal glory in Christ, after you have suffered a little while, will Himself restore you and make you strong, firm, and steadfast. To Him be the power for ever and ever. Amen. (1 Pet. 5:1–11, NIV)

As you pray for Christian, I have a new word to help direct your requests, fragile.

All of our boys have been big babies. Christian was over nine and a half pounds when he was born. But as we held him today, it is obvious that he is fragile. Much of his energy is spent either breathing or fighting off the infections. While we know that it is a miracle that he is still even with us, it is difficult to see him so weak. Please ask God to bestow on Christian the blessings of strength and health. Ask Him to remove these infections from Christian's body and restore him.

Please keep Margaret in your prayers, as well. She has been bothered with frequent dizziness, probably from a sinus problem. Please join me in asking God to remove this discomfort so she can focus on caring for her family.

Lastly, please continue to keep Margaret and me in your prayers. We have been asking ourselves some difficult questions: Can we trust God even if His answer does not match our desire to see Christian healed? Will we still lean on Him as we look toward Christian's lifetime needs for special care? Our faith is being put to the test and we need God's grace and mercy more than ever. We continue to look to His Word and make it our desire to draw close to Him.

Thank you and God bless you.

DCE

Saturday, June 21, 2003, 11:50 PM

All,

Well, it has been five days since Christian was extubated. PRAISE GOD! He continues to improve.
Thanks for your prayers!

DCE

Monday, June 23, 2003, 11:50 PM

All,

Christian's recovery is slow, but it's still a recovery. Today, Margaret fed him about 6cc of breast milk from a bottle. He was able to suck and even swallowed. It was very exciting. Margaret spent much of the day with him, holding him and rocking him. He has become *clingy* and now notices when Margaret is leaving.

Please continue to pray that God would heal Christian from his infections. The doctors are still trying to get the correct antibiotics for the strains of infection that he has. In addition, they are concerned with the condition of his kidneys. Also pray for his stamina. Although six cc is a good start, he needs to be able to drink more and for a longer period of time.

> The Spirit also helps our weakness; for we do not know how to pray as we should, but the Spirit Himself intercedes for us with groanings too deep for words; and He who searches the hearts knows what the mind of the Spirit is, because He intercedes for the saints according to the will of God. (Rom. 8:26–27)

Thank you for your prayers and for being a blessing to our family.

In His care,

DCE

Margaret's Journal

June 25, 2003

Dear Lord,

Praise God that on Monday I was able to feed Christian his first bottle. He drank six cc of milk. Then he was tired and went to sleep. Yesterday, he was able to drink about twenty cc in one sitting. He was very cute and cried for more (little whimper cries) and then I would let him suck a little longer. So he was *nippling* for about twenty minutes. He was a little cranky after—maybe gas or he was tired.

Today, he had another PIC line put in his leg and a line put in his head. He doesn't look so well, but he must feel OK tonight. Today, when I held him, he smiled at me three times. It was so cute! Then he was tired but no cry today.

Praise God! Yesterday, our Pastor Paul prayed over Christian and today Bernie prayed for us at the boy's swimming lessons. Also, Audrey came to visit us at the hospital.

Amen.

Wednesday, June 25, 2003, 11:58 PM

All,

I want to begin by thanking you for your prayers, your words of encouragement and experience, and your concern and care for our family. God is using many of you to speak to us and we appreciate your willingness to share.

Christian continues to make some progress. He was able to take a little milk from a bottle yesterday. This is a huge blessing and we are hopeful that he will be able to take the vast majority of his calories and nutrition orally. Another blessing was that Christian smiled at Margaret three times today. This was even more special since he had a rough day today.

The doctors were concerned enough with Christian's kidneys that they ordered a CT scan to get a good look at them. We have not heard back on the results. While they were doing the scan of the kidneys, they decided that they might as well scan the whole body, so that will give the doctors an opportunity to get a good look at him. In addition, Christian had to have two IV lines replaced, one of which required some sedation and a trip to the cath lab. As a result, he did not get to eat today until after 5:00 PM.

Christian is still fighting infections and the doctors are still trying to find the most effective treatment to deal with them. Please pray that God would simply remove this affliction from him.

Most of the doctors and nurses have commented that Christian is a good-natured child and, despite all that he has to put up with, usually is quite sociable. We are grateful that he has a patient personality and a sweet spirit. Praise God.

In His care,
DCE

♡❃ Margaret's Journal ❃♡

June 26, 2003

Praise God!
I can hold him.
He is gaining weight—now 5.12 kg.
For our medical insurance.
No oxygen is needed today.

CHAPTER 8

The Marathon

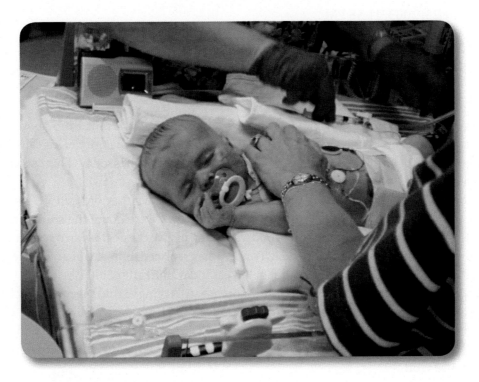

Saturday, June 28, 2003, 11:03 PM

> Sing to Him a new song; Play skillfully, and shout for joy. For the word of the Lord is right and true; He is faithful in all He does. The Lord loves righteousness and justice; The earth is full of His unfailing love. (Psalm 33:3–5, NIV)

The last few days have been very busy for us. The pace has been a little frantic and we are exhausted. Despite the need for sleep, we have much to be thankful for:

Praise God that Christian is able to get fed from a bottle twice a day.

Praise God that Margaret and I get to be the ones that feed him.

Praise God that Christian's blood cultures are beginning to come back negative for at least one of his infections.

Praise God that Christian is not having serious symptoms of the infections.

Praise God for the opportunities to hold Christian frequently this week.

Praise God that Christian's lungs are working well.

Continue to lift up Christian to God. Ask for the blessings of health and strength on his road to recovery. He still has another couple of infections to overcome, and he needs to gain weight and strength to help him developmentally. On Monday, the doctors will take a closer look at his kidneys with a white blood cell scan to determine if there is any cause for concern. Pray that Christian's kidneys will show up perfectly healthy. Ask that God would put a hedge of protection around him to protect him from any attacks, whether physical or spiritual, that might sabotage his recovery.

I would like to ask you to bring some fellow patients before our heavenly Father to ask for His blessings of healing. Kimberlee, Brandon, and Andrew are Christian's roommates, and they need an extra measure of God's grace as they recover. Their recovery has been difficult for them and for their families. Also, continue to keep Cara and her family in your prayers. She is continuing to struggle and her parents need rest and peace right now.

> To Him who is able to keep you from falling and to present you before His glorious presence without fault and with great joy, to the only God our Saviour be glory, majesty, power and authority, through Jesus Christ our Lord, before all ages, now and forevermore! Amen. (Jude 1:24–25, NIV)

Thank you for your support and care and especially for your prayers. They are a blessing and a hope to my family. We are seeing the glory, majesty, power, and authority of God daily and we continue to praise Him.
God bless and keep you.
DCE

Monday, June 30, 2003, 11:53 PM

> To pray is to change. Prayer is the central avenue God uses to transform us. (Richard J. Foster, *Celebration of Discipline*)

I find it interesting that Margaret and I have spent the last year making a concerted effort to improve our communication with God. Prayer had become a ritual and not a very consistent one at that. When reminded about the blessing of bringing our praises, requests, and thanks to our loving and gracious Father, we made a commitment to come before him unceasingly as a couple and as individuals. We had no idea what He was preparing us for.

> Don't fret or worry. Instead of worrying, pray. Let petitions and praises shape your worries into prayers, letting God know your concerns. (Phil. 4:6, The Message)

We will not worry about Christian or about the future of our family. Instead, we bring our requests and praises to the sovereign God:

- We ask that You would bring peace, rest, and comfort to Christian as he sleeps tonight.
- We ask that You would protect Christian from spiritual or physical harm.
- We praise You for the healing work that has been done so far.
- We thank You for gifting so many people with the experience and skills necessary to provide Christian with competent care.
- We thank You for Christian's smiles.
- We thank You for choosing to expand our family.
- We again commit ourselves to the task of bringing up Christian, Jordan, and Brenton to be Godly men.
- We ask that You would grant our boys health, peace, and Your grace.
- We ask for Your blessing on those who receive this message.

In the name of Your Son, Jesus Christ, our Lord and ever-present Saviour,
Amen.
DCE

Wednesday, July 2, 2003, 11:56 PM

All,

I want to thank you for continuing to pray for Christian. We have been spending more time with him since he is so alert and social.

We were happy to hear that Christian's white blood cell scan showed that there is no evidence of infection and his latest blood cultures show no sign of infections. We thank God for this blessing and pray for His protection from disease for the remainder of Christian's stay at the hospital.

Christian continues to drink from the bottle two or three times a day. We are hopeful that he will be able to nurse this week.

We ask God for Christian's complete healing and that He would allow Christian to come home soon. Thank you for joining us in this prayer.

God bless you.

DCE

Friday, July 4, 2003, 11:26 PM

All,

The last few days have been a real blessing to Margaret and me. We have been able to hold him regularly, feed him from a bottle, make him laugh, and give him a lot of positive (non-painful) attention. He is a joy and has been very patient throughout this experience. It has been very difficult the last couple of nights to leave him because he has been so alert and playful. Praise God for this wonderful child!

We spoke briefly with the doctors today, and they are sounding upbeat. The big milestone right now is for him to be able to eat regularly and fully from a bottle. He is currently drinking 20–40 cc from a bottle before he is just too tired to continue. He needs to be able to drink at least 65 cc (a little over two ounces) every three hours. Pray that God would give Christian strength and stamina to complete his feedings, gain weight, and get stronger.

We haven't heard much about the infections. The doctors will continue to keep Christian on antibiotics throughout the month to make sure there is no opportunity for him to get another infection. Please ask God to protect Christian from further infection and to withstand the effects of being on antibiotics for so long.

We continue to ask God for complete healing. We lay at His feet our desire to have Christian come home soon.

> Hear, O Lord, and have mercy on me; Lord, be my helper! You have turned for me my mourning into dancing; You have put off my sackcloth and clothed me with gladness, To the end that my glory may sing praise to You and not be silent. O Lord my God, I will give thanks to You forever. (Psalm 30:10–12, NKJV)

God bless you.

DCE

Monday, July 7, 2003, 10:57 PM

Friends and family,

Christian is ten weeks and four days old today. The time is really going by fast. This experience is so unlike anything we have ever gone through or expected to go through. But we realize that we are in the company of people who are suffering and in need of a great deal of comfort. We see hope in Christ's words:

God blesses those people who depend only on Him. They belong to the kingdom of heaven. God blesses those people who grieve. They will find comfort! God blesses those people who are humble. The earth will belong to them! (Matt. 5:3–5, CEV)

Please pray for God's blessing on these families that are enduring so much.

We are thankful that Christian continues to recover. He is consistently gaining weight (up to 10 pounds, 1.5 ounces, today), drinking regularly from a bottle (up to 40 cc), and interacting well with his surroundings. He has been giving his mom and dad some smiles and seems to be content only when in our arms.

There are still some milestones that Christian needs to reach. He has developed some lung congestion and will be given some medication to get rid of any fluid accumulating in the lungs. He is being weaned off the remaining morphine dosage and may go through some withdrawal symptoms. He is still on antibiotics, which can be hard on the digestive system, but it looks like the infections (except the yeast infection) are gone. There is a good possibility that Christian will be moved to the recovery ward this week, which is also a good milestone to achieve.

Continue to keep Christian in your prayers. Also, keep Margaret and me in your prayers. As we see the approaching opportunity to take Christian home, we also see the transition we need to make. There is a steep learning curve in caring for a child with heart disease. Ask that God would give us the grace to get through this phase, through the transition, and into a routine at home. Thank you all for your prayers, your help, and your encouragement. You are a blessing.

In Christ's care,
DCE

Wednesday, July 9, 2003, 11:46 PM

All,

Christian continues to slowly improve. It is easier for us to see that he will be coming home soon. We praise God for watching over this little boy.

Given the condition of the other children in Christian's room, it can often be a stressful place to be. Pray for peace.

A hospital is a busy place and there is a lot of active equipment, which amounts to ambient noise that can be quite high. Pray for rest.

While the frequency of various *care tasks* has decreased, there are still many times when Christian is subjected to uncomfortable procedures and intrusions. Pray for comfort.

Thank you and God bless you.

In His care,
DCE

Friday, July 11, 2003, 12:03 AM

Christian had a rough day today. The fluid in his lungs has turned into serious congestion and it is playing havoc with his breathing and oxygen saturation. The doctors are doing a lot of investigation to see what might be causing it.

Ask God to give the doctors wisdom as they find a treatment for Christian. Pray that Christian will be able to rest easily tonight and be free from the discomfort of his deep cough. Pray for his healing and peace.

Thank you all.

In His care,
DCE

Friday, July 11, 2003, 10:24 PM

All,

Please continue to pray for Christian. The doctors have said that he has a type of pneumonia. They have adjusted his antibiotics to account for the possibility that this may be bacterial pneumonia. If it is viral pneumonia (like a really bad cold), then all they can do is give him respiratory treatments to keeps his airways clear of congestion. He has a bad cough and gets congested very easily. He has not had any milk from the bottle since Wednesday because of this. All his feeding has been through his NG tube.

We are asking that God would give Christian the rest necessary to fight off pneumonia and give him comfort as he suffers through yet another difficulty. We are also asking God to grant Margaret and me peace in the midst of this stress and faith to see that God is in control.

God bless you.

In His care,

DCE

Monday, July 14, 2003, 11:31 PM

> I sought the Lord, and He answered me, and delivered me from all my fears. They looked to Him and were radiant, and their faces shall never be ashamed. This poor man cried and the Lord heard him, and saved him out of all his troubles. The angel of the Lord encamps around those who fear Him, and rescues them. (Psalm 34:4–7)

Fear is a difficult thing for us to master. We fear the unknown, the future, the past that might be revealed, our loss of control, and for some of us, enclosed spaces. But two things are true about our fears. First, they are our own; second, we can be delivered from them. My fears are that I will not have the stamina to see this experience through or that I will not be able to accept the outcome. The reality is that I don't have the stamina or the ability to accept. But I have to trust that God will deliver me from these fears and equip me to stay the course and accept His will. So I will lay face down and wait for His rescue.

Christian is slowly recovering from pneumonia. The doctors think that this is just viral pneumonia since none of his cultures have come back positive for bacterial growth. This is a blessing despite the discomfort Christian is going through. Yesterday, they decided to increase his sedative dosages to ensure that he would rest, the only way to recover. Margaret spent most of Saturday with him so I could spend the day with Brenton and Jordan. On Sunday, we all went to visit Christian.

Christian needs to get over this pneumonia so that he can start taking his feeds orally again. He has been taking his milk through his NG tube since he gets congested easily. He also needs to gain weight every day, a milestone for recovery. Furthermore, Christian is on quite a bit of medication, much of which he will have to be taken off of before they can remove his single IV line.

Please, continue to request that God would bring about complete healing of Christian's body and that He would allow us to take Christian home soon. Pray that Christian would continue to grow physically and developmentally. And ask that God would give the doctors wisdom to find the best way to get Christian off the medications while still providing him with what he needs.

Once again, Margaret and I are so grateful for the support you have shown to us. God uses you to encourage us when we are down and provide for us when we are weak. Whether it was a card, a hug, or a listening ear, we have received them just when we needed them. What a gracious God and what faithful people! God bless you.

Still in His care,

DCE

Wednesday, July 16, 2003, 10:32 PM

All,

    I would like to ask you to pray for a couple of things:

- Margaret is really struggling physically and emotionally with the stress we are under. Her back has been really bothering her, making it difficult for her to rest. Furthermore, she is torn each time she has to leave Christian. If one of us is not there to comfort and hold him, the only way he gets the rest he needs is to be sedated. Ask that God would give her physical comfort and peace of mind.
- I have asked before that you would hold Cara, the nineteen-year-old who is also recovering from heart surgery in your prayers. I would like to ask all of you to take a moment to commit her to God right now. She is in need of complete healing and her parents need to be held tightly in His hands. Go before God on this family's behalf.

God bless you.
In His care,
DCE
(Cara passed away shortly after this email was written.)

Sunday, July 20, 2003, 10:18 PM

All,

    This has been a good weekend for Christian. He continues to grow and heal. Gradually, he is being taken off of medications and having tubes removed. Best of all, he has been smiling. We know we are blessed to have this wonderful gift of a son. Our hopes this week are that he would be moved to the recovery ward. Furthermore, we hope to have a conference with the doctors and care staff to discuss Christian's progress and what we need to do to prepare to care for Christian at home.

    While Christian was having a good day today, the rest of us had a difficult start. On the way to church, we were hit from behind by another driver. Margaret was already taking a pain reliever and was even using an ice pack on her back while in the van. This trauma just added to her discomfort. When we got to Stanford, we made a quick visit to Christian and then spent two and a half hours in the emergency room to make sure we did not have any serious injuries. There was no extensive damage to our van, but we will have to go through the insurance hoops to get the claim settled. We thank God for keeping us from greater harm and ask for his wisdom as we deal with the consequences. Furthermore, we are asking that God would extend his healing to Margaret's back.

    We thank God always for the people He has put into our lives to care for us, pray for us, encourage us, and love us. God bless you and keep you.
DCE
Psalm 121

Wednesday, July 23, 2003, 10:53 PM

All,

    The last couple of days have been pretty exhausting for the family and I am worn out, so I will make this short.

    We had a *care conference* today with the hospital staff to find out the next steps for Christian. The staff was very positive about the possibility of getting Christian home by early August. There are a couple of issues that still need to be brought to the Lord in prayer.

First, while he is gaining weight (praise God), he is not taking enough food orally. Because of this, Margaret and I need to decide if we will be bringing him home with an NG tube (through the nose to the stomach) or a G-tube (through his side into his stomach). Neither options are permanent but will be necessary for a while. The G-tube requires minor surgery, and he will need to be intubated for the duration of the surgery. Margaret and I are hesitant about subjecting him to another surgery, even a minor one. The result, however, is that Christian would be free from any tubes around his nose and mouth, which would help him learn how to take his food orally. Ask that God would grant us wisdom to make a good decision and peace once the decision is made.

Second, Christian will need to start his vaccinations. Not only will he need his regular vaccinations (polio, meningitis, etc.), but he will also need to be vaccinated against various respiratory illnesses. His condition puts him at higher risk if he catches these diseases. Ask that God would prepare Christian's body for these vaccines and protect him from any adverse side effects from them.

Finally, pray for Margaret. She is in a great deal of pain and needs rest. Her back seems to be getting more irritated and inflamed. Ask that God would extend His healing hand to her body.

Thank you for your prayers and your messages of encouragement. You are a blessing.

In His care,
DCE

Sunday, July 27, 2003, 10:23 PM

> I am still confident of this: I will see the goodness of the Lord in the land of the living. Wait for the Lord; be strong and take heart and wait for the Lord. (Psalm 27:13–14, NIV)

I am fortunate in that I have seen the goodness of the Lord in the eyes of a thirteen-week-old child in the acts of supportive friends and in the answered prayers of so many faithful people. Until I leave this life to spend eternity with my God, I am grateful for these glimpses of His character. Thank you, God, and I continue to wait for You.

We continue to wait for God's timing in Christian's recovery. This weekend started out a little rough as Christian was having trouble keeping his food down and had some reaction to his first vaccinations. However, I just got home from spending a few hours with him and he was content, interactive, and happy. Praise God!

Margaret and I think that it would be better for Christian to have a G-tube for feeding. This direct connection to his stomach will allow us to teach him to nurse or drink from a bottle while still meeting his caloric and volume needs. The plan is to have him checked out by the GI (gastroenterology) team to assess his condition and schedule his surgery. Please pray that Christian will have the strength for this surgery, that the surgery will go well, and that this will help him get the nutrition he needs.

It was good for Margaret and me to spend some time this morning worshipping with friends and finding encouragement and strength with fellow followers of Christ. Know that God is using you to minister to us and give us hope. May God richly bless you.

In His care,
DCE

 Margaret's Journal

July 29, 2003

Dear Lord,

Last Thursday, Christian turned three months old in the hospital. Wow! This is a mixed blessing. We praise God that he is alive after so much, but we are sad to still be separated as a family. He is far away from us each night. We feel so far and distant. Sixty-four miles round trip from our house. I can never get there fast enough. I have cried a tear for every minute I have been apart from him. We are still on the roller coaster ride. Thank You for all the many people still reaching out to us. It is a blessing. Lord, bless all the people who have helped take care of Brenton and Jordan. I have missed being with them every day of this summer (and spring). It has been the most difficult time of my entire life. Dear Jesus, we pray you would also bless Christian's life as he is growing. Thank You for the many smiles he has given me. It is so hard that I have to share them with dozens of people each day. I long to be with him alone. I pray that he would be able to bond with me and feel close and secure. I pray that Your Holy Spirit would give him that security. Please fill that void.

Thank You that many of my prayers have been answered. Thank You that we have been able to hold him again and again, to change his diaper, to sing to him, to hear him cry, to see his smile, to try and nurse him, to bottle feed him, and to burp him. I just didn't realize we would be doing all of these things in the hospital. Lord, I pray You would bless all the hands that have cared for Christian. They are so numerous. There are more people than I even know. Thank You, Lord. I pray that I might go home soon so we can miss the staff at the hospital.

Continue to strengthen me, Lord. I cannot do this on my own. Continue to supply me with milk for Christian. Bless his body and make him whole again.

Praise God. Today, Christian was able to drink again from a bottle (95 cc). What a miracle. He was so satisfied with the first bottle, and peaceful, too. The second bottle, he had to work harder for. Lord, we pray that this would get easier for him so he might be able to take more of his feeds orally. We are still deciding on the G-tube or not this week. It looks like we will need to take him home with an NG tube or a G-tube.

Thank You for the continued weight gain. Christian is 11.3 pounds! Lord, help us make the final decision about what would be best for Christian. I know many nurses recommend the G-tube, but I just want to be sure that this is best before we do it. Lord, please show us what is best for Christian's needs before we do this surgery. Amen.

CHAPTER 9
Out of CVICU

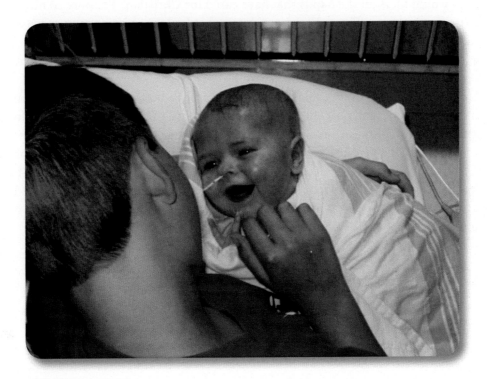

Thursday, July 31, 2003, 11:00 PM

Today, Christian is fourteen weeks old. He continues to gain weight and will be taken off four antibiotics. We are hopeful that he will be taken to the recovery ward this weekend or early next week.

The doctors are concerned that Christian may have a fungus in one of his kidneys (they are not absolutely sure, however). They have decided to start him on two weeks of anti-fungal medication. Unfortunately, he will have to remain in the hospital while this course of medication is completed. Please pray that his kidneys would clear up without any side effects from the medication.

> But as for me, I trust in Thee, O Lord, I say "Thou art my God." My times are in Thy hand. (Psalm 31:14–15)

Thank you for your support and love. God bless you.
In His care,
DCE

 Margaret's Journal

August 2, 2003

Christian had a great day. He nursed for ten or fifteen minutes with much crying, but he did get satisfied and go to sleep.

August 3, 2003

Good day. He did not want to latch on—he wanted to sleep in my arms and suck the pacifier. He also did not take the bottle from David or me. He took it once from the nurse.

August 4, 2003

He had a good night's sleep, the nurse (Mark) said. The doctors keep talking about sending him upstairs (to recovery). We are praying that today will be the day, if it is Your will, Lord. We have talked about it for many weeks.

We are going to take two more weeks for anti-fungal treatment. They said that the ultrasound showed that the kidneys were not clear. One is clear and the other still has something there—maybe a fungal ball. The doctors do not know what it is and they do not all agree that it is a fungus. Lord, I know You know and we pray that You will work at healing Christian's body so he might be united with us at home. We pray that your healing hand would work a miracle through these doctors and nurses. Amen. God bless today.

Tuesday, August 5, 2003, 6:58 AM

All,

I realize that I haven't sent out an update lately. The number of updates recently is inversely proportionate to the time we have been spending at the hospital. In fact, I am at the hospital right now (I was able to find a network connection to use). So here is what is going on.

On Friday, we were told that Christian was looking very good. While the doctors are still concerned about one of his kidneys, they did not see anything that would keep him from going up to the recovery ward (third floor). The two-week treatment he is on for his kidneys could just as easily be administered upstairs.

Margaret and I were able to spend a lot of time with Christian over the weekend since we stayed in a local hotel. Most of the time, he rests. However, we have been able to feed him orally more often and that is encouraging. Because of this, we have decided to postpone the PEG (G-tube) surgery. We want to spend the next few weeks working on his oral feeding and possibly forgo that option. He continues to gain weight (over twelve pounds now) and tolerate his feeds.

At around noon on Monday, the staff moved Christian to a room on the third-floor recovery ward. On the positive side, this is a big step toward his homecoming. On the negative side, it was a larger step than we expected. He is no longer under constant observation by the nurses. Instead, it is expected that there be a parent or other caregiver in the room with him twenty-four hours a day. This will certainly prepare us for when Christian comes home, but it will require that I spend the night with Christian for the next couple of weeks.

Thank you for your constant prayers and for the care and support you have so graciously given to us. Continue to keep Christian and our family in your prayers. We are asking God to clear up Christian's kidney. We are also asking God to show us the best way to ensure that Christian continues to be well-nourished. Finally, we are asking God to give Margaret, Brenton, Jordan, and me endurance for, what we hope, is the final stretch in Christian's current stay at the hospital. We thank you for joining us in bringing these requests to our loving Father in heaven.

Let me shout God's name with a praising song, let me tell His greatness in a prayer of thanks. (Psalm 69:30, The Message)

In His care,
DCE

Wednesday, August 6, 2003, 10:59 PM

All,

We thank God for the people He has put into our lives to carry us through this difficult period. Thank you for your sacrifice of time and energy to care for us and to show us, such love. You are a blessing.

I have a couple of requests that I ask you to bring before our heavenly Father. First of all, it appears that the medication that Christian is taking for his kidney needs to be taken for four weeks, not for the two weeks we were originally told. However, the doctors have told us that they will take another look at his kidney in two weeks and let us know if there is an improvement. If there is, they might let us take him home early. What we are asking God for is complete healing of his kidney by the time they check it again, with no further need for medication.

Secondly, please pray on behalf of Margaret. She continues to battle back pain to the point where she was unable to get to the hospital today. Ask that God would heal her back and protect her from any further affliction.

Again, thank you for your love and support. May God bless you.

In His care,
DCE

Saturday, August 9, 2003, 5:34 PM

All,

Christian has been having fevers periodically and was having trouble keeping his food down the last couple of days. The doctors did a urine test and found a bacterial infection. He will have to be put on an antibiotic.

Just when we seem to be making headway, we get news like this and it makes it difficult for us to see when we can bring him home. Please ask God to strengthen us and show us hope.

God bless.
DCE

Wednesday, August 13, 2003, 5:01 PM

I took Christian down to radiology this morning for an ultrasound of his kidneys. After a few minutes of looking around, the radiologists came to the conclusion that Christian's kidneys look good and clear. There is no evidence of any fungal infection.

Thank God for His healing mercies.

As a result, Christian was taken off one of his IV medications. Today or tomorrow, Christian's blood will be checked to see if the other infection is growing. If it is not, he will be taken off the remaining antibiotics by this weekend. Please continue to pray that Christian's body will be free from any infections. Once he is off of the antibiotics, Christian should be able to come home. This is the desire of our hearts and our constant prayer.

Thank you for bringing our requests and for bringing Christian before our gracious God in prayer. We are seeing His hand at work.

God's blessings on you.

In His care,
DCE

CHAPTER 10

Home

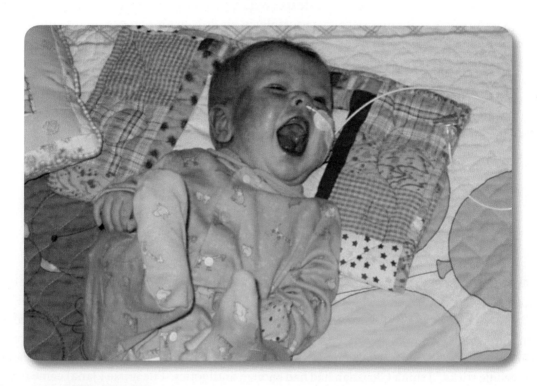

Friday, August 15, 2003, 8:42 PM

All,

This has been a good week for Christian. He continues to gain weight and take much of his food orally. He has been sleeping well and has been interacting well with his nurses and visitors. We know we are blessed to be at this point in his life.

Christian has had an IV up to this point so that he could continue receiving antibiotics. The plan was to continue his antibiotics until tomorrow morning. This afternoon, however, the IV came out, and rather than put a new one in, the staff decided he had had enough antibiotics. Praise God.

On Sunday, some of Christian's blood will be drawn and tested. If his blood shows no signs of infection after twenty-four hours, he will be discharged. This means that our son could be home as early as Monday. Again, give praise to God.

Please ask God to protect us from any spirit of fear. We don't know what to expect when we get him home: how to protect him from sickness, how to make sure he is eating enough, how to sleep and still listen for his breathing. We want this to be a joyous occasion for our family as we will be united for the first time in our own home. Ask that God would grant us courage.

This weekend will be busy as we prepare for Christian's homecoming. We still have a few more skills to learn and a crib to build. We ask for God's peace amidst the excitement.

We thank you for your prayers and encouragement. We are more confident knowing that you are interceding for us.

You who revere the Lord, trust in the Lord; He is their help and their shield. (Psalm 115:11)

In His care,
DCE

Monday, August 18, 2003, 11:37 PM

Nearly seventeen weeks ago, we laid at the feet of our heavenly Father our desire to bring Christian home with us. As I write this, Christian is sleeping peacefully in his crib, in his home, with his family.

We serve a loving God who chose in His mercy to give us the desire of our hearts. We praise Him for keeping us in His care and for giving us His strength for this adventure. We rest in this truth. We know that whatever situation God allows us to be in or specifically puts us in, He will provide us with the grace necessary to get through it and the opportunity to give Him glory in it (see Rom. 8:28; 1 Cor. 10:31; 2 Cor. 12:9).

Thank you for giving us so much encouragement. God bless you.

Still in His care,
DCE

♡❋ Margaret's Journal ❋♡

August 22, 2003

Dear God,

On August 13, they did an ultrasound of Baby C's kidneys and they said they looked alright. The doctor came in and said good work. I told him it wasn't me. Praise God! We just needed to wait for the infection in his blood to clear. We prayed day and night. We had hundreds of people praying for his healing! On Saturday, we were hoping they would do a blood culture and that it would be negative. His last antibiotics would be on Saturday.

On Friday, August 15, his IV came out. I couldn't believe it. I told David, "Please don't let them give him any more needle sticks." I think Christian had had enough antibiotics. The nurse (Jana) came in and agreed. She said they would not reinsert the IV. That was such a blessing.

On Saturday, the boys came to the hospital all day with me to see David and Baby C. It was a very good day and my mom and dad came to see him, too. They babysat Christian while we went out to Chevy's with Brenton and Jordan for dinner.

On Monday, the very special day came. We prepared to go home. They said at 3:00 PM, we would be discharged after all the paperwork. Yeah!

I had to learn on Sunday how to put in the NG tube before we left the hospital. I did it. The nurse (Megan) was very helpful and she suggested that I wrap up Baby C first so his arms would be still and she held his head. It was difficult emotionally, but it went well.

We have been home for four nights. I am beginning to get more tired. It is very difficult to keep pumping milk now that Christian is home. He has so many special needs. Lord, I never expected this. I knew he would have recovery after his surgery, but I had no idea what his special needs would be. Lord, thank You that David has been able to help me so far. I pray that I would be able to get the help I need this year. Lord, I want to still be able to homeschool Brenton and Jordan. I am not sure how this will happen. Lord, please make this clear to me.

We are praying for Baby C's special need to learn how to drink his bottle. He has forgotten how to suck. He is not able to take any food orally. Lord, my prayer is that he could take all of it orally through a bottle. Amen.

Saturday, August 23, 2003, 10:07 PM

Praise God! This is our sixth night at home with Christian. His older brothers are having a great time entertaining him and helping Mom and dad care for him. For the first time since Christian was born, we feel whole as a family. God has richly blessed us.

Christian hasn't broken the thirteen-pound mark quite yet, but we continue to work on it. We have had to make some adjustments so that we could get larger blocks of sleep in the evening. We were hoping that, once at home, Christian would really take to nursing or at least, to the bottle. On the contrary, he eats even less by mouth. As a result, we use a *kangaroo* pump to give him his feeds through his NG tube. This is very disheartening for Margaret. We are in the process of arranging to have a therapist work with Christian. We pray that Christian will not lose his motivation or skill to take his food orally.

While Christian is strong, he missed quite a bit of his physical development while in the hospital. We are working a little with him, but we will need to be more proactive with this. Pray that we can find just the right physical therapist to work with him and that he would get stronger.

Finally, we are asking God to grant Margaret and me stamina and physical strength as we adjust to Christian's new schedule. We had expected frequent feedings and all the other typical changes that come with a new baby. However, the NG feedings and the medication schedule have made things a little more complex and require us to be more lucid in the middle of the night. So far, I have lost about three ounces of milk on the floor while priming the tubing for the kangaroo pump. I'm just not at my best at three o'clock in the morning.

We thank you for your prayers, notes and phone calls of encouragement, and for your time and talent in caring for our family. God has truly used you to be Christ to this family. God bless you.

In His care,

DCE

♡❀ Margaret's Journal ❀♡

August 28, 2003

Dear Lord,

Last Saturday, we were able to celebrate Jordan's seventh birthday at Grandma Dana and Grampa Mike's house. Thank You. That was special. On Wednesday night, we were able to celebrate with Nana and Papa at our house. Mom brought the dinner (ham, salads, bread, and cake with strawberries). She is amazing. It was all delicious, of course. She brought presents for Jordie and it was special. Baby C stayed in his swing for dinner time.

On Sunday, I took the big boys to church. David stayed home with Christian. Afterward, I went to the mall for lunch and then shopped for Brenton and Jordan. It felt great to be out and know that David was with Christian the whole time. Thank You for the blessing of us all being together as a family. It has not been easy these past ten days, but it has been a blessing to be united. It is a special gift that all sleep under the same roof and wake up to see each other. Thank You that I don't have to call the hospital to see how Baby C is doing. We can just get up and look.

We are still trying to adjust to being the only ones caring for Christian. I was really used to the nurses and doctors helping with his medicines every day and all of his feeding preparation. I must pump each bottle, then label and put away (freezer or refrigerator), then measure for feeding and add formula, try to have him nipple a while, measure the remainder, and then transfer it to the feeding bag with the kangaroo pump. Give us strength, Lord, to feed him day and night. Help me to know how much to give him and when. Help Baby Christian to keep gaining weight. He was at thirteen pounds the last time he was weighed. We also pray for his right eye. It has a clogged tear duct and some discharge. We pray for healing.

Today, we saw the new occupational therapist, Carol Black. Lord, we need another miracle. He is still not taking any milk orally, only a few cc's now and then. The goal is 680 cc a day.

Thursday, September 4, 2003, 1:02 PM

Christian has been home for eighteen days! Praise God!

We thank God that Christian is slowly gaining weight (he is over thirteen pounds now).

We thank God that Christian continues to take some food from a bottle.

We thank God that Christian is getting to know his brothers.

We thank God that Christian gets to be in a home environment.

We thank God that Christian is able to get out and about every so often.

We thank God that Christian is getting stronger.

Since Christian has been home, we have been trying to get into a schedule for eating, medications, appointments, schooling, rest, exercise, and so on. So far, that schedule has eluded us. Christian and his brothers are getting the attention they need, but Margaret and I are not sure when we are supposed to eat or sleep. We realize that it may take a little more time to finally get into a schedule that works for all of us.

There are a couple of things you could pray for. First, Christian still needs to be able to take all his milk from a bottle since he refuses to nurse. Right now, he continues to get about 60 percent of his food through his NG tube. This is becoming more problematic since he has pulled the tube halfway out twice and all the way out once. We are working with a therapist to improve his feeding skills. Ask God to bless the time we are spending with the therapist, that Christian might improve.

A second area for prayer is that Christian has developed some rashes, along with conjunctivitis in his right eye. This has made life a little uncomfortable for him since we have to put his hands in *mittens* to keep him from scratching his face (and from pulling his NG tube out). Some of the rashes are normal baby stuff, but some are due to medications. We will be seeing a pediatrician today to find a way to treat these. Ask that God would relieve Christian of this discomfort.

Lastly, we will be seeing Christian's cardiologist tomorrow. This will be the first time since Christian has left the hospital. We are a little apprehensive about the visit because we don't know how well Christian has healed. Ask God to give the doctors wisdom as they evaluate Christian and ask God to grant us peace during this visit.

Thank you for your prayers. Thank you for your care and support.

May God bless and keep you.

In His care,

David

Sunday, September 14, 2003, 11:46 PM

Continue to keep Christian in your prayers. We are struggling to help him gain weight and we are back to the question of having him in for surgery to get a G-tube. Ask God to grant us wisdom.

God bless you.

DCE

♡❋ Margaret's Journal ❋♡

September 17, 2003

Dear Lord,

Tomorrow, Christian will have been with us for one month! Praise God! We are still adjusting to all of the changes in our family. Lord, bless us and keep us in Your care. It is not easy. The days are sometimes very difficult. It is wonderful to have Brenton and Jordan's help each day, but it is also hard because I feel like they need more structure for learning. Lord, please provide a way for them to go on field trips this year. I will really miss not being able to be involved. The summer was really hard to miss, also. I look forward to doing things with them that are fun someday. Please provide a way for me to do that. I look forward to us being able to go out as a family again someday. Lord, help us care for Baby C each day.

Our goal now is to feed Christian between 700 cc and 835cc each day. Help us feed him enough to reach our goal so he can gain weight. He is 13 pounds, 10 ounces. I pray that You would help him gain an ounce a day. Give us guidance about the way we should handle the feeding tube. Help us, Lord. It is so hard. Please comfort us. Amen.

Wednesday, September 24, 2003, 11:37 PM

In God we make our boast all day long, and we will praise Your name forever. (Psalm 44:8, NIV)

We thank God for His mercy on our family. We praise Him for giving us these last five months to get to know this wonderful little boy we named Christian. We ask for the Healer's gentle touch on Christian's body as he continues to grow and gain strength. We ask that God would grant us many more months and years to spend with the newest member of our family. Our hope is that the world will see the light of Christ in this little boy's life.

Amen.

Sunday, October 5, 2003, 10:13 PM

All,

Well, Christian has been home for seven weeks and we praise God that he continues to grow and develop. The task of caring for him, however, is more daunting than we had anticipated. There is the constant struggle to keep him from pulling out his NG tube and the difficult ordeal of reinserting it when he does. We ache to see his skin worn out from the adhesive tape that holds the tube and the rashes that he gets from his medications. This little boy continues to go through suffering, and it is difficult to see relief. Please bring Christian before our Heavenly Father and ask that He would comfort our son and bring healing to his body.

Margaret is under a great deal of stress right now. The lack of sleep from attending to Christian and the need to care for all three boys are wearing on her. To add to the stress, I will be having outpatient surgery on Tuesday that will leave me unable to lift anything for about three weeks. We are asking God to protect her mind and strengthen her body and give her a spirit of peace. We are also asking that God would bring healing to my body by whatever means He chooses.

Margaret and I cannot thank you enough for the support over the past few months. Many of you have given and continue to give sacrificially of your time and resources to care for and love our family. We thank God continually for the blessings of friends and family.

In His care,
David

May the God of hope fill you with all joy and peace as you trust in Him, so that you may overflow with hope by the power of the Holy Spirit. (Rom. 15:13, NIV)

Friday, October 24, 2003, 12:42 AM

All,

On Friday, October 24, Christian turns six months old. Thank You, God, for giving us this time with Christian.

Christian continues to adjust to life at home. He is taking more formula orally and is gaining weight. He has figured out how to move about on his back and can roll over on his side. He loves to be entertained by his brothers and is usually at peace when in his mother's arms.

While Christian has made quite a bit of progress, he is still struggling to keep much of his food down. Also, it is difficult to keep him from trying to pull out his NG tube or rub off the tape that holds it in place. It is very annoying for him and frustrating for us. We have decided to heed the doctor's advice and proceed with surgery to deal with these issues.

The current schedule is for Christian to go into surgery on November 10 (this date can change as it has already) at Lucile Packard Children's Hospital to have a G-tube placed in his abdomen and for him to undergo surgery to correct a reflux problem he is struggling with. The surgery is laparoscopic but will still require a hospital stay of approximately three to four nights because of Christian's heart condition.

We know that the surgery is necessary, but the thought of him being intubated, anesthetized, and in CVICU (for one night) is a little hard for us to see positively. We feel like we just got him out of the hospital. We hate to send him back. Furthermore, because of Christian's particular heart condition, the risks are greater.

Continue to keep Christian, as well as the rest of our family, in your prayers. The time leading up to the surgery date can be difficult and we have a tendency to let our emotions overwhelm and rule us. Furthermore, we have removed Christian's NG tube temporarily to give his face a rest from the constant taping needed to keep it in place. This makes it a little more difficult to make sure he gets enough to eat and to make sure he receives (and keeps down) his medications.

Please ask God to grant Margaret and me an extra measure of His strength at this time. I am still recovering from a surgery I had on October 7. Because of this, Margaret has had the extra burden of physically caring for Christian without me giving her a break. Also I ask that God would continue to watch over Christian and that He would use the surgeon's skills to correct the problems Christian is dealing with.

We thank God for His mercy and for giving us His wisdom as we find the best ways to care for and treat Christian.

Proverbs 8

God bless you and keep you.

In His care,

DCE

CHAPTER 11
Back to the Hospital

Tuesday, November 4, 2003, 11:56 PM

Friends and family,

I would like to ask you to pray for Christian. He has an appointment with a dermatologist at Stanford because of his extensive rash. The rash may keep Christian from having his surgery on Monday. We have a number of concerns. We obviously don't want Christian to go into surgery with any added risks due to his rash. At the same time, we are anxious to relieve Christian of the NG tube, which just plays havoc with his skin and sinuses. After the dermatology appointment, Margaret will see the surgeon to discuss whether or not to proceed with the surgery.

Please keep Christian in your prayers—that he would be calm on the way to and from the hospital and during his appointments, that his rash would just clear up, and that the surgery would go smoothly. For Margaret, ask that God would give her peace and clear thinking tomorrow as she speaks to the doctors and staff.

Thank you for your prayers and for the constant support these past months. We are blessed to be the recipients of your love and support.

In His care,
DCE

Saturday, November 8, 2003, 11:54 AM

All,

First, I want to thank all of you for keeping Christian in your prayers. We heard back from many of you that you would bring these requests to our Heavenly Father on behalf of Christian. This means a great deal to us and is honored by God.

Second, I want to give you the results of our doctor visits. As you know, Christian is scheduled for surgery on Monday to have both a G-tube inserted (for feeding and meds) and to correct a problem with reflux. Christian saw a dermatologist and a surgeon on Wednesday to determine if his rash would prevent him from having surgery. The surgeon did not think that we would need to postpone the surgery and we could proceed safely. Furthermore, the dermatologist prescribed two skin ointments to treat the rash and praise God, Christian has improved dramatically.

Yesterday, we went in to see Christian's GI doctor to find out if the reflux surgery will be necessary. She evaluated the amount of food he is taking in and keeping down, the concentration of the formula, and his rate of weight gain. She was not convinced that Christian can keep enough food down without the reflux surgery because he is still not taking in enough food, the food has not had enough calories, and he is not gaining weight fast enough. However, over the weekend, she wants us to try giving him about thirty-five ounces in twenty-four hours of a more concentrated formula to see if he tolerates it. If he does, she feels reasonably confident that he can do without the reflux surgery.

Please join me in praying for Christian:

Heavenly Father, we thank You for the gift of Christian and for choosing to expand our family. We thank You for letting us get to know this little person for the past six and a half months. We praise You for all the miracles that we have seen in his life in that time. We bring Christian before You and commit his life to Your loving care. Father, we ask that You would strengthen Christian with the food that he takes and allow his body to gain the full benefits of its nourishment. We ask that he would be able to take what he needs regularly and that he would not require extra surgery for his stomach. Father, as we prepare Christian for his surgery on Monday, we ask that You would prepare the medical staff. Give them rest and peace. Father, we ask that You use the staff's skill and experience to do the best job possible and we ask that You give them Your guidance while Christian is in the hospital. Father, grant Christian the blessings of healing and strength for this next week and allow us to bring him home quickly and safely.

Father, we lay these praises and requests at Your feet because You commanded us to and because we know that You hear them. We bring them before You in the name of Your Son, Jesus. Amen

Acts 3:16
DCE

Monday, November 10, 2003, 7:33 PM

I will give you thanks in the great assembly; among throngs of people, I will praise You. (Psalm 35:18, NIV)

Margaret, the boys, and I have much to be thankful for today!

We worked with Christian this weekend to see if he could tolerate more food and at a higher concentration. Praise God, he was able to take OVER the amount that the doctor said he needed for two days. Because Christian was able to take this much volume without any reflux, we decided not to have him undergo corrective surgery for the reflux.

This morning we came to Packard Children's Hospital and let the surgeon know our decision. This threw a little wrench in the works. Because we were not trying to have two procedures in one surgery, there were more options for having the G-tube placed. This resulted in several conversations among the doctors and with us that ended up delaying his surgery a little. The extra wait was a little too much for Christian, and he ended up being quite agitated when he finally went in.

After about an hour, the surgeon came out to see us and let us know that the surgery went well. In addition, the cardiac anesthesiologist was satisfied that Christian was doing well enough to bypass any time in the CVICU and go straight up to recovery. While he is in the constant observation ward of recovery, I am still staying the night to keep an eye on him. The surgeon is confident that Christian will be able to go home tomorrow. That is our hope.

Praise God that Christian was able to take an increased volume of food without any reflux problems.

Praise God for the wisdom and skill He gave the medical staff at this hospital.

Praise God that Christian's surgery went without incident.

Praise God that Christian is no longer using an NG tube (the one through his nose).

Praise God for His comfort and healing mercies to Christian.

Please continue to lift up Christian in your prayers. We ask that God would comfort him in his pain. We ask that he would heal quickly and be able to take food soon. We ask that he would be able to come home tomorrow.

Thank you all for your support and for your diligent prayer. We know how much God delights in hearing the praises, thanksgiving, and requests of His people.

In His Care,

David

Tuesday, November 11, 2003, 10:00 PM

All,

I want to thank you again for your prayers, encouragement, and help. Christian is still at the hospital. The doctor decided to observe him for one more day to see how well he tolerates food. So far, he is doing well and we anticipate that he will be released tomorrow (11/12).

God bless you.

In His care,

David

 Margaret's Journal

November 11, 2003

Dear Lord,

Yesterday, Christian had his G-tube surgery. Thank you that it is over with. Help him to recover well from the surgery. His skin is healing well from the severe eczema that he has. Thank you to Dr. Lane, the dermatologist.

Help me to get over the shock of Christian's health problems. It is so difficult for me to see him not heal quickly. He is very slow to gain energy. He has not been able to *thrive* or gain weight. Last month, he did not gain very much. He kept losing weight. He did keep growing in length. It is so hard with his heart. It seems like every week we increase the volume of milk we give him and every week he weighs between fourteen pounds, thirteen ounces and fifteen pounds. One day, he weighed fifteen pounds, five ounces. We were so excited and then he dropped again. Yikes! This is so difficult.

Lord, I pray You will help him tolerate his formula. Help him to take the bottle well again and increase his food intake. Lord, I will give You all the glory. He needs to become stronger to sit up. Lord, I pray You would help him gain strength in his back to sit and stand someday. Right now, it is a dream and a prayer. Lord, You are able. Thank You that You have helped him make so much progress. Lord, please continue to work in Christian's life. Surround his room with Your angels tonight at LPCH. Bless the babies that are sharing the room with him.

Comfort me tonight and comfort David and keep him warm in the hospital. Give Christian good rest and sweet dreams. Amen.

Wednesday, November 12, 2003, 3:55 PM

Praise God! Christian is back home!

He is still recovering and is still in some pain, but he is eating and interacting well. Thank you for your prayers and for praising God with us.

David

Psalm 9:10–11

Margaret's Journal

November 16, 2003

Dear God,

Are you there? I am not sure. I know that Christian came home from the hospital and that was an answer to our prayers. However, I realize that he is not gaining enough weight. Lord, we thought that we did not need to do the reflux surgery. We prayed about it. We thought You gave us a clear answer. I am crying right now because I have seen Christian vomit every day since he came home from the hospital. We need help. We need guidance. Baby C is not improving and he is not getting enough volume. Lord, I pray You would help find a solution that is not surgical. I don't know how to care for Christian, Lord. We need Your help.

Lord, help me. I am being emotionally tormented. It is so hard to find all the support I need. I know friends do not know how to help. I don't know what to say. I miss having time with friends and their kids. I miss going to church and other places as a family. I am so sad and so stressed. I must care for Christian. I don't know how to care for my health. Give me the strength, God. I am losing the desire to do anything. I don't feel like eating or doing anything in the garden. I don't have the strength to go shopping. I don't feel like doing school because I am so busy caring for Christian.

I feel like I never get to talk about anything with David. Our relationship is strained. Lord, unite us in our marriage. We are being put through a terrible test. Life is upside down—nothing is normal. It feels like nothing will ever be the same. I want to be able to help others and be a friend to others and have other kids over to our house. I wish I could have get-togethers with other families, and I wish we could go to Nana and Papa's house as a family. I miss that. Lord, please end Christian's suffering. Please help him to grow and be strong. Amen.

November 17, 2003

Dear God,

Thank You for sleep and rest. Thank You that I could wake up and see Christian and David sleeping peacefully together. That is a gift from You. Thank You for the smiles that he was able to have yesterday.

I pray that You would bless his day and we pray for healing still from Christian's surgery. There was redness and we are not sure what to do. Please help us to see a doctor if needed today.

Amen.

Sunday, November 23, 2003, 11:30 PM

All,

I realize that I tend to get these emails out when we are in the most need. The reality is that the last couple of weeks have been very stressful and Margaret, and I have not had much sleep. Since Christian came home on November 12 after having his G-tube surgery, he has been having a lot of trouble keeping his food down. We thought it would improve as he healed and that he would be able to take the same amount of food he took before the surgery. Instead, it became increasingly difficult for him to keep his food down. This weekend, things began to get dangerous as he was not only losing his food but his medications, as well. By this morning, he was obviously sick and getting dehydrated. The doctors recommended that he go to the emergency room at Stanford. After spending about four hours in ER being observed and investigated, it was decided that Christian should be admitted. They are treating Christian for gastroenteritis and reflux which has led to dehydration. We expect to be in the hospital for a few days.

Our family is dealing with a variety of things right now. Brenton and Jordan have been concerned about their little brother and were worried about him going back to the hospital. Margaret and I are stressed after dealing with two weeks of Christian's inability to keep food down. Margaret's stress is manifesting itself as doubt and anxiety while I am finding myself frustrated and angry over the situation. Please ask God to give us peace right now—to keep our eyes on His Son, Jesus, and not give in to the surrounding storm.

Please ask God for His healing mercies on Christian. Our desire is to see our son able to fend off minor illnesses and to develop into a healthy little boy. Pray that God would use the talents and wisdom of the doctors here to treat Christian and be the instruments of his healing. Thank you for keeping us in your constant prayers.

In His care,

David

 Margaret's Journal

November 24, 2003

Dear Lord,

Praise God, Christian is seven months old today. The part that is hard to praise You for is that he is in the hospital. Yesterday, we took him to the emergency room (Sunday afternoon) and had him admitted. He has not been tolerating his milk since he had his G-tube placed. Lord, please show us Your plan.

Lord, I hate the family separation. I pray You would bring us family unity again. Unite us, Lord. I feel a real battle taking place. I feel like we are fighting so hard to keep our family of five altogether. Lord, hear my cry. I pray You would provide a way for us to go places as a family together—someday soon.

Lord, bless David and Christian at the hospital tonight. Watch over Christian Jr. and help him tolerate his milk. Lord, give us wisdom and the doctors wisdom, too. Please, help CJ (Christian Jr.) get stronger, too. He is so beautiful. Thank You for all seven months. Lord, bless his life and glorify Yourself through him.

Amen.

November 25, 2003

Dear Lord,

Baby Christian is still in the hospital. Today, he was moved to an isolation room. Lord, we have so much concern about him. We pray for the protection of his physical body. He is very sick. I pray his body would be able to fight the germs. Help us know what is best. Give us wisdom. Please, give us good doctors. Lead us to the right formula for his body to gain nutrition and gain weight. We are desperate. He is very underweight.

Thank You for the blessing of praying and meeting with people today. We met another family with a little girl named Melissa (who is four years old, now), who also has heart disease. Her mom, Tammy, went to school with David. It was neat to hear about the miracles in their lives. Tammy is a cancer survivor and has had two children since. God bless them and their three girls.

Thank You that I met Mike, our garage door man today. He has a little girl Kristen. We pray for all of her health problems. She has many problems with her brain and has seizures. Lord, I pray for that family. The wife is an occupational therapist named Kathleen. I pray that if it is Your will that we talk and meet, that You would work that out.

Lord, may Your will be done in Christian's life this week. We are very sad to all be separated. I pray, if it is Your will that we are together as a family of five or all the family for Thanksgiving, please provide a way for us to spend some time together. Bring back the joy, Lord. Please, give us peace and rest.

Amen.

PS: It was good to see that baby Nicole was doing well. God bless her. Help her to get off oxygen.

Thursday, November 27, 2003, 11:46 AM

> Now He who supplies seed to the sower and bread for food will supply and multiply your seed for sowing and increase the harvest of your righteousness; you will be enriched in everything for all liberality, which through us is producing thanksgiving to God. For the ministry of this service is not only fully supplying the needs of the saints, but is also overflowing through many thanksgivings to God. (2 Cor. 9:10–12)

All,

Our family usually has much to be thankful for. We have been the recipients of God's providence and mercy over the years, and we praise Him for His faithfulness. This year, we are especially thankful for the gift of Christian and that he gets to celebrate this Thanksgiving holiday with us. We are also thankful for those of you who have given so much to our family. Your generosity has been a blessing to us in so many ways.

After nearly four days in the hospital, Christian was discharged last night (11/26). The doctors were able to rehydrate him and get him back to the weight he was last week (which is still underweight). They adjusted some of his medications and we tried some different formulas to see if he could tolerate his food a little better. Please continue to pray for him. We don't feel that we have yet found the right mix of medication and formula that will allow him to get the calories that he needs without side effects or allergic reactions.

Thank you for your support and prayers. May God grant you peace in the name of His Son, Jesus Christ, and by the power of the Holy Spirit.

In His Care,

David, Margaret, Brenton, Jordan, and Christian

♡❀ Margaret's Journal ❀♡

November 27, 2003

Dear Lord,

Thank You for the extra Thanksgiving blessing. Thank You that Christian was discharged from the hospital last night. I had no idea they would release him after three nights. Lord, it was so scary. I thought it could be more days or weeks if he was put in isolation. We pray, Lord, that You would continue to heal his body and help him to tolerate formula. Help us through these difficult times. Help Christian to get enough nutrition to grow. We praise God Christian is home. Now, help us to care for him.

Amen.

CHAPTER 12
First December

♡❀ Margaret's Journal ❀♡

December 3, 2003

Dear Lord,

Fill every empty space inside me. Fill me with Your Holy Spirit. I am overwhelmed with sadness and stomachache when I wake up still. "Nothing is impossible with You" (Luke 1:37). I know that You can help me face Christian's feeding issues today. Give him the strength to drink his bottle. Give his body the ability to digest his food quickly. Help him to gain weight today now that he is home from the hospital. I pray that You would work a miracle today, and You would help Baby C tolerate all his milk.

Amen.

December 4, 2003

Dear Lord,

Give me strength for today. Give me peace and help me to care for Christian. Today, he has a GI appointment. I am not sure if Baby C is improving. Last week was very difficult to be in the hospital. Thank You for the blessing of being home.

Lord, I pray that his home care and circumstances would improve. He is still not tolerating his food really well. He is taking much orally and keeping it in longer, but the stomach is still erupting like a volcano. We have changed to Prilosec, a GI medication that helped at night. Lord, give us wisdom. This is the hardest situation I have ever had in my life. Help me to get him to the doctors today. I don't want him to miss any food time.

Lord, we need supernatural intervention. No human doctor can fix everything. Lord, I pray that You would intervene and have Your healing hand on Baby C. Help him to tolerate the amount of milk he needs—at least 1,040 cc a day—like he did before the G-tube surgery.

Thank You for all the blessings and help You have given us. We praise God little Melissa Garrison is home from the hospital. I pray her oxygen saturation (sats) would go up.

Amen.

Saturday, December 20, 2003, 12:32 PM

Merry Christmas!

This year you will probably receive a number of Christmas/New Year's letters that are humorous, informative, or just convey greetings. This note is going to be celebratory. We have much to celebrate.

Most importantly, we praise God for the gift of His Son, Jesus Christ. C.S. Lewis once wrote that "God is both further from us, and nearer to us, than any other being." It is a miraculous event that the Creator of the universe would incarnate Himself—become a man to live on this earth—in the person of Jesus Christ simply because He loves us. That fact alone is enough for me to clear my schedule for a day just to ponder the boundless love God has for us.

Praise God for allowing us to witness the miracle of Margaret's pregnancy and the birth of our third son. We had "stepped out of the boat" when we asked God to bless us with a larger family. On April 24, we welcomed Christian Elias Ekstrand into the world. We were surprised to find that this blessing came with some special needs. After spending a total of eighteen weeks in the hospital on three separate occasions, we have a greater appreciation for the privilege of parenting and a greater admiration for those parents who seem to live at hospitals in hopes of seeing their child healed.

We praise God for leading us to the fellowship of believers at Christ Community Church four years ago. It has been a place of healing, renewal, learning, and support for our family. This year, in particular, we have experienced the providence and mercy of God through his obedient servants. We are further blessed by the families from our support groups that have shown such great love and sacrifice in caring for us.

We praise God for our families. This has been a busy year in terms of medical needs, and our parents have been a great source of support and love. We have been able to depend on them to watch (and occasionally teach) Brenton and Jordan, provide meals, stay with us in the hospital, and check up on us regularly. We are so blessed to have our families close by, especially at this time in our lives.

Praise God that Brenton and Jordan have had an opportunity to get to know their little brother. They have been caring, entertaining, helpful, and loving with Christian. It is truly a joy to see the three of them together.

We praise God for the gift of marriage. This has been a difficult and stressful year for us. It has taken great effort to find unity and stability in our circumstances. But God has been merciful and has continued to knit us together as we come to His throne with our needs.

We would ask that you continue to keep our family in your prayers. We look to God for healing, for unity, for peace, for courage, and for joy.

> And the peace of God, which surpasses all comprehension, will guard your hearts and your minds in Christ Jesus. Finally, brethren, whatever is true, whatever is honorable, whatever is right, whatever is pure, whatever is lovely, whatever is of good repute, if there is any excellence and if anything worthy of praise, dwell on these things. (Phil. 4:7–8)

We hope that your celebration of Christ's birth will be joyous and may God bless you in the new year.
In His care,
David, Margaret, Brenton, Jordan, and Christian

CHAPTER 13
New Year

♡❀ Margaret's Journal ❀♡

January 18, 2004

Dear Lord,

Thank You that Baby C was home with us for the whole month of December. Praise God! He was home for his first Christmas!

We celebrated Christmas Eve here as a family of five. We had chicken and dumpling soup and then opened presents. We could not make it to church this year. We missed having Nana and Papa here for our celebration. They were very sad not to be with us. Mom had the flu this year and was so concerned that Baby C might get it.

Praise God Mom and dad were able to come over last weekend to celebrate with us. It was enjoyable and very special. They came on Saturday afternoon. We cooked tamales that were in the freezer, beans, rice, salad. Mom brought fruit salad and angel food cake with strawberries. We took many pictures and made many memories.

Praise God! Amen.

January 19, 2004

Dear Lord,

Thank You for the blessings of our family. Thank You that we were able to go to Valley Fair on Saturday and have lunch as a family. Thank You that we went to San Jose History Park and Brenton worked on his history project and I was able to feed Christian his bottle. Thank You that he was able to take it so well. Thank You that he tolerated most of it.

Thank You that on Sunday, David was able to go to church and take Jordan. After church, we all went for a ride and Brenton videotaped the old route for the San Jose Alum Rock train to the park for a history project. Thank You that David is able to teach him that. I pray that You would continue to help us teach the boys. Give us wisdom and guidance. Bring peace to our home so that it might be a better learning environment for Brenton, Jordan, and Baby C.

Lord, help us to have a special day on Christian's first birthday. Lord, I pray for much progress over these next three months. I pray that he would be healthy so we can enjoy a celebration as a family and maybe even with friends.

February 2, 2004

Dear Lord,

I have prayed many nights and days since I have written. Last week, I had a terrible cold virus. So did Brenton and David. Now, Jordie is feeling a bit sick today. This week, I am struggling with insomnia. It is awful. I have been waking up at about 4:00 AM and not able to go back to sleep after that. Why, Lord? I spend time praying—but then I still cannot sleep even though I am very tired! I need the gift of sleep, Lord. I beseech You. It affects my whole day.

We have been praying for Baby Christian about his G-tube. He now has a staph infection. Lord, I pray that the topical antibiotic would help.

We are having problems with insurance coverage. Please help Baby C with the transition to the new reflux medication. It is hard to make the change on his body. The Prilosec is $150 per month. The insurance company will not pay for it. Praise God, Mom gave us $500 for Christmas that will cover his 2 hospital visits in November and part of one bottle of medicine.

Help me to manage this household. It has been very stressful lately. Lord, I pray You would bring peace and joy to our lives. Bring healing to David today. He had another endoscopy on his throat. He has the third one in two months. We pray for improvement, Lord. We need Your healing hand.

Help me to be able to sleep in the same room as David again. It has been months. We pray for Your mercy. Baby C is still on the feeding pump at night and sometimes in the day. It is still very challenging for me. I can only do it each day with strength from God. I do not have extra help, yet. I don't feel like I have enough support for our family. Please help me figure out what to do. It is so hard. I can't even express it in words to most friends. It seems like more than most friends can take. That's just the physical part—not even the emotional part.

We need to fill out paperwork for respite care. Please help me to accept help. I feel like I will lose all privacy. I don't even enjoy having my mom fold my laundry or bring Baby into the bedroom. It is so messy, Lord. I don't know how to manage more people, Lord. Yikes! Help me, Jesus!

Continue to show us Your presence, Lord. Please relieve me of the tension in my body.

Thank You that Dana and Mike were able to help with David. Thank You for Brenton, Jordan, and Christian.

Fill me with Your Holy Spirit.

I feel empty.

Amen.

February 17, 2004

Dear Lord,

I have just a few minutes before I need to give Baby C his medications. Yesterday, David and I were so tired that we both forgot his morning medications for the first time.

Lord, we praise You for all that You are doing in our lives and in Christian's life. Thank You for having Your hand on his health. Help me to keep looking to Jesus and not at Christian's problems. I pray that You would continue to give David and me strength to care for all three boys. We know they are such a blessing.

Thank you for the miracle that we were able to go out to dinner on a date last night! Dana and Mike watched the boys and Baby C. We went to Milpitas to Dave and Busters for dinner. It was very nice. We needed to go somewhere without a long wait. It worked out well. Dana is about to have surgery on her knee, so soon she will not be able to help.

Lord, continue to give Baby C strength in his muscles and help his development. He cannot sit up on his own or roll very well. He is not crawling or walking. It is so hard to think about. I pray that he will continue to make progress each day. Thank You for the physical therapy.

Amen.

PS: Thank You that on February 8, he was able to go to church with us as a family for the first time! We pray we could go on a more regular basis. Help to work out his feeding problems, Lord, so that he can grow and develop and go more places with us.

February 22, 2004

Dear God,

Many blessings today! Thank You. Praise God. Friday, my mom was able to take Brenton to his first overnight camp at Mt. Hermon. Our church leaders organized a great event (fourteen leaders went). Yeah! Lord, bless them.

Yesterday, Jordie had his friend, Brian, sleepover. It was special because it was just the two of them (twenty-four hours).

Christian made it to church with us and we went out for lunch to the mall AND we saw his old nurse, Tracy. What a surprise from God. It was a reminder from You of how far Christian has come and how well he is doing. Tracy could not believe how big he was. God, bless her. Amen.

Wednesday, February 25, 2004, 12:07 AM

All,

Christian turned ten months old today. We celebrate this milestone because we recognize God's mercy in allowing him to be with us. Christian has been home with us for six months now. He is growing stronger and is getting chunkier. He is usually full of smiles and loves laughing with his brothers. It is a joy to spend so much time with him.

His last few doctor's appointments have been very encouraging. We have a new cardiologist and he was very pleased with the function of Christian's heart. He has already started to take Christian off some of his medications. What a blessing! His GI doctor was very pleased with Christian's weight gain and is happy to see him thriving. Christian continues to get physical therapy, and our hope is that his upper body will be stronger.

We continue to praise God for Christian's progress and for the many people that have supported us for the last several months. While we know that we still have a difficult road ahead, we know that God is faithful and that we can trust in His grace, provision, and strength.

Because of the Lord's great love we are not consumed, for His compassions never fail. They are new every morning; great is Your faithfulness. I say to myself, "The Lord is my portion; therefore I will wait for him." (Lam. 3:22–24, NIV)

In His care,
David

 Margaret's Journal

February 25, 2004

Dear Lord,

Today was an all-day ordeal to feed Christian. I was emotionally, physically, and spiritually challenged. Please bring me peace of mind tonight. I felt like I hardly had a minute to breathe. I tried to homeschool Brenton and Jordan but felt very unsuccessful at it.

There went the timer for the feeding pump! Time is up, God. Lord, I am always out of time. I was never able to even call a friend today, it was so stressful. Lord, have mercy. It seems like nothing went as planned today.

March 14, 2004

Dear Lord,

Today was a pretty good day, Lord. We thank you for the many blessings. Today, I was able to go to church and worship with Brenton and Jordan. Then, I went home and picked up David and Christian. We went to the celebration for Graham Clark. He returned from Iraq two weeks ago. We thank You for bringing him home safely. We praise You for watching over Julie and the kids while he was gone for one year. Unify their family again. Bring peace to their home. Protect them from any spirit of destruction or anything unclean.

Lord, these past few weeks, we have much to be thankful for. Last week, Dana had knee replacement surgery. She seems to be healing well. We praise You for no infection. Last weekend, we were able to spend some family time at home and at the mall. Baby C seems to do pretty well in his stroller.

On March 3, according to Dr. McCracken's scale, Baby C weighed in at twenty-two pounds! We praise God. That was so wonderful and I had tears in my eyes when I called David to tell him the news.

Things are a little less emotional these days. Sometimes, I still start to cry about all that we have been through. If I think of a song, such as "Twinkle, Twinkle Little Star" or something that we have not done since Christian was in the hospital, I get emotional. When I realize that every day is still a gift from God, I get tears.

I have a hard time reading about the heart. It is difficult because there is no quick fix to Christian's problem, yet. The doctors still do not know how to *fix* his heart. I pray that someday, they will find a way to repair his heart so that he does not have to be a single-ventricle patient.

Lord, it was good to call Tami and David Garrison to see how Melissa is doing. David said that she is still having low oxygen levels, in the 70 percent range, which is the same as before the surgery. That was not very good to hear. It was good to hear that she feels OK and that she is going to travel to Disneyland next month. Melissa is four years old and plays just like all the other kids. We pray that You would continue to bless her. We look forward to seeing them again. Keep Melissa in Your care and we pray for continued improvement in her physical health.

Lord, continue to help Baby C develop physically. He is sitting with support every day, but he needs help sitting. Without support, he can sit for two or three minutes at most. Help him learn to be mobile; give him the motivation to explore and strengthen.

CHAPTER 14

Spring

♡❋ Margaret's Journal ❋♡

March 20, 2004

Dear Lord,

Praise God. It's the first day of spring! Thank You! We have much to be thankful for today. Yesterday, Baby C went to see Doctor Grady, the cardiologist. He said C weighs 22 pounds, 9 ounces and was 31 inches. His sats were 75 percent–82 percent. His blood pressure was OK. His heart rate was in the 140s. We are very thankful for all the weight gain. He said C was like a little piggy. He is still on the feeding tube at night. We hope someday and pray, Lord, that this is just a part of the past. Help him to be able to make progress and take more baby food and table food. We pray that, through the power of Your Holy Spirit, Christian would be healed of this acid reflux problem. We pray he would outgrow this very serious condition. Continue to help him through each day when he is having difficulties. Help him not to suffer.

We thank You, Lord, that I was able to run into baby Max. It was a blessing to see Cynthia, his mom, and to see that Max looked good. Last November, Christian and Max were in the same room together and very sick.

I read on the web about hypoplastic left heart syndrome (the heart disease similar to Christian's) this week. It was a blessing to read about other people's journeys—Cameron and Joshua. Praise God for bringing them this far.

Amen.

PS: Lord, we thank You for Dad's seventieth birthday. We celebrated today at Nana and Papa's. Today was Baby Christian's first time for a dinner visit to Nana and Papa's house. Praise God!

March 24, 2004

Dear Lord,

Praise the Lord. Christian is eleven months old today. When I first spoke those words this morning, Baby C got sick all over me and the chair. Ugh!

We thank You, Lord, that on Sunday, Christian was able to go to church with us as a family again (the first time in March). Afterward, we went to Baja Fresh for lunch and he did very well. Praise God! I was able to go out and shop while David stayed home with the boys. Thank you for that time out.

Lord, continue to give David strength for his job. I know he is working so hard at home that he hardly has time to rest. Help him to be very productive at work.

Praise God! Yesterday, Paula was able to come and pick up Jordan and take him on a field trip to a play—*The Hobbit*. Also, Nana and Papa helped us. My dad came to babysit Jordan after the play and Nana went with Baby C and me to Dr. Trager at noon. Baby C did very well at the appointment. He was twenty-two pounds, twelve ounces. Thank You, God. We did one immunization (HIB) and ordered the RSV. Lord, I pray that the vaccinations would not hurt his body in any way. Help him to tolerate it and become stronger.

PS: It was good to talk to Tammy. Praise God, Melissa is still doing well. She is back at preschool and potty training when on Lasix (every other day). Bless her.

Tuesday, March 30, 2004, 11:39 PM

All,

Christian is eleven months old!

We say this with the deepest gratitude for how God has blessed our family. It certainly hasn't been the easiest eleven months, but we are learning to take each moment one at a time. Christian had appointments with his pediatrician, his cardiologist, and his GI doctor this month. We are happy to report that all three went very well. The doctors are pleased with his progress and happy with the function of his heart. We are getting a little more relaxed not having to watch his food intake or his color so carefully. At this point, our biggest concern is his reflux and his physical development. Please pray that he can get over these hurdles.

Next month, we look forward to celebrating Christian's first birthday. We have much to celebrate! We are also planning to have a baby dedication. Our church gives parents an opportunity to publicly commit and bring up our children to follow our Lord, Jesus Christ. For us, it is also an opportunity to present him to our church family and celebrate God's mercy and grace on our family.

Again, we thank you all for your prayers and support these last eleven months. We have seen God's hand daily as He works through you.

Oh, give thanks to the LORD, for He is good! For His mercy endures forever. (1 Chron. 16:34)

DCE

♡❀ Margaret's Journal ❀♡

April 1, 2004

Dear Lord,

It has been challenging these past few days. We were home all weekend, no family outings. Baby C still has a cold virus. Lord, please heal this virus. Cleanse our home. Continue to help him to breathe well. We went to Homerun Sports on Monday. Christian was a little fussy, but it was OK. It was very windy and cool that day.

Baby C made it to physical therapy on Tuesday. It went really well with Scott, the physical therapist. On Wednesday, we decided to go to the Marleys' house. Our small group usually meets, but no one can meet. So we enjoyed finally getting together with Greg and Andrea. Then today, Janet, the occupational therapist, came to work with Baby C.

Tomorrow, Praise God, Mom might come with me to go see Dr. McCracken, the GI doctor. Lord, protect my mom and strengthen her. We pray that the visit will be helpful and positive.

Lord, I ask that You would heal my tongue and mouth (sinuses). I have sores under and on top of my tongue. It is very painful and difficult to eat, drink water, or talk. Lord, please heal me.

Lord, watch over Brenton and Jordan tomorrow. They are going on a field trip to San Raphael to a guide dog center. We pray for protection.

Amen.

April 6, 2004

Dear Lord,

Praise God, Christian was raising his arms up more this week.

Praise God, he was able to wear his overalls this week.

Praise God, he is rolling the ball back and forth a lot.

Praise God, we made it to church as a family on Sunday and were able to go to the mall for lunch and shopping (even though he had sickness).

Praise God, Baby C was twenty-three pounds, six ounces and thirty-two inches long last Friday.

April 20, 2004

Dear Lord,

Praise God, David had a vacation last week!

Praise God, we went to three fun places with the boys and church for Palm Sunday and Easter Sunday.

Praise God, Baby C was twenty-three pounds, eleven ounces at Dr. Trager's office on Tuesday.

Praise God, we had some rest.

Praise God, David and I had two dates on vacation. Nana and Papa babysat one time and Grandma Dana and Grampa Mike babysat the other time. It was hard to leave Baby C, but we really needed it.

Praise God, I made it through another rough day today.

April 24, 2004

We praise God we celebrated Christian's first birthday with the family. We had a BBQ. My mom brought green salad, corn salad, deviled eggs, fruit salad, and delicious coffee cake. Dana brought macaroni salad and drinks, and we provided pork and chicken. We had a chocolate birthday cake with a Pooh Bear candle.

Afterward, we celebrated by opening a mountain of presents with Christian. He enjoyed it, too.

David showed our video of Christian and shared it with everyone. It was very special. It was a very special evening, and we praised God for bringing us through the year and for the gift of life.

We were also excited to find out that Mark and Maureen are expecting a baby in October. We pray that this baby will be very healthy and strong. God bless their growing family.

Sunday, April 25, 2004, 12:57 AM

All,

It has been a long year for Christian. It is bad enough to have to leave the safe and comfortable confines of the womb and be thrust (literally) into an unsafe and complicated world. But to make the transition more difficult, he has to struggle through two surgeries, many days in the hospital, and two sleep-deprived parents. What's the point?

There are those who say that we are the result of millions of years of chance occurrences and unmanaged chemical reactions. The obvious conclusion to this naturalistic view is that we exist and then we don't and that there is, ultimately, no point—no purpose.

I reject this notion as unreasonable. The complexity of the universe that I can observe implies that it was designed, and therefore the result of some intelligence. The fact that it exists implies a willful decision on the part of a personal being. If an intelligent personal being took the time to design something as large and complex as the universe, it is reasonable to assume that there is some purpose to it.

Given this, I have to conclude that the last year was not without purpose. In the 138th Psalm, the author, King David, makes this statement, "The Lord will fulfill His purpose for me; Your love, O Lord, endures forever—do not abandon the works of Your hands" (NIV).

I have yet to figure out why God allowed Christian to have heart disease or why our family had to endure a stressful twelve months. I can be sure, however, that it is not without purpose. God may, in His mercy, reveal that purpose to Margaret and me in our lifetime, or we may have to wait until we see our Savior, Jesus Christ, face-to-face to get the answer. But we can rest in the assurance that the intelligent, personal, Creator God does not make mistakes, neither does anything happen in the universe outside of His control.

As we celebrated the first anniversary of the birth of our third son, we also celebrated the purpose for which he was entrusted to us, his parents. We trust that God will bring about that purpose and that, someday, God's name will be glorified in the life of Christian Elias Ekstrand.

God bless you.

David

CHAPTER 15
Lessons Learned

There may be some of you who have while reading this book asked why? Why is Christian having to suffer through heart surgery and recovery? Why does this family have to go through this ordeal? Why does any family have to go through this kind of ordeal? Why do bad things happen? In a couple of years preceding Christian's birth, I had been studying the problem of pain and evil in the world. The study had been predominantly philosophical and academic. All of a sudden, my study had become more practical.

Less than twenty-four hours after Christian was born, I was faced with a difficult decision. The doctors at LPCH evaluated Christian's condition after looking at his heart and after using a catheter to keep the blood flowing to his body and lungs temporarily. The doctors were now ready to make some recommendations. My father was with me as they explained the options. The first option was to take Christian home to die peacefully with his family. Given his condition, death was a medical certainty if no further measures were taken.

The second option was a heart transplant. This was obviously a drastic measure but not uncommon. The chances of a successful heart transplant were about 50 percent-60 percent, provided a suitable donor heart could even be found.

The last option was a series of no less than three open-heart operations that would reconfigure Christian's circulatory system. These operations did not carry the risk of transplant rejection, but the procedures were relatively new. The chances of surviving all three operations were about 50 percent.

Although I was thankful that medical science had advanced to a point where these options were even available, I was angry. This is not the kind of decision I thought I would have to make. To make matters worse, I would have to present the options to Margaret who was still recuperating from the birth in another hospital. This was the most difficult decision we had ever had to make as parents.

I was angry that God had put me in a situation where none of my choices were particularly promising. There was no scripture that said, "As a follower of Christ, you should _____ when your son has heart disease." Margaret and I knew that no matter what option we chose, we would always be tempted to question our decision.

So why would God put us in such a situation?

Part of the answer to that question struck me when Christian was two years old and needed another catheter procedure. This would be different from his previous procedures because he would be far more aware of what was going on. As we took him into the room to prepare him for this procedure, for which he would have to be anesthetized, he was unable to understand the necessity of it and the various painful experiences that were part of the package. It was difficult for me to console him, to assure him that I loved him, to calm his fears, or to let him know that he would get through this. Most of all, I was unable to impart to him how important this procedure was to his survival on this planet. And then I realized that God was trying to communicate the same things to me.

I cannot see the *big picture*, but God can. I cannot know what is in my future, but God does. I cannot hope to answer all of the why questions, but God has the answers and will give them to me when He thinks I am ready. Just as Christian has to trust that I want what is best for him, I have to trust that God wants what is best for me.

Another part of the answer might be in the decision Margaret and I made three years ago. After spending time studying God's Word and after much prayer together, we knew it was important that we trust God with our family planning. We had seen how God was using parenting to shape us into Christ-followers that had to depend entirely on Him. We knew that allowing God to expand our family would provide even more opportunities for God to mature us in our faith. Was this also part of God's answer to our prayer? Did we inadvertently bring this upon ourselves? The reality is that it is more difficult for me to be shaped into the man God wants me to be when things are going well. When things are not going according to my own plans, I am forced to mature and become what God wants me to become.

Despite these possible answers, I still cannot tell you why Christian was born with a heart that doesn't work well. While I might someday discover the physical reasons for the defect in his heart, I probably won't have all the answers as to why Christian had to suffer through this. And I don't know how I will be viewing this five, ten, or thirty years from now.

Is it wrong to question God—to question the Creator of the universe? It's not. However, it is wrong not to listen to His answers.

When we felt at our lowest, we looked to God's Word. When we rejoiced with every little gain, we looked to God's Word. When we felt alone, in despair, hopeless, joyful, grateful, we looked to God's Word.

In Paul's second letter to the church in Corinth, he wrote:

> But we have this treasure in earthen vessels, so that the surpassing greatness of the power will be of God and not from ourselves; we are afflicted in every way, but not crushed; perplexed, but not despairing; persecuted, but not forsaken; struck down, but not destroyed; always carrying about in the body the dying of Jesus, so that the life of Jesus also may be manifested in our body. (2 Cor. 4:7–10)

The biggest temptation Margaret and I faced and continue to face in our circumstances is to believe the lie that God will crush us and leave us in despair. That is not how God treats those who have put their faith in His Son, Jesus Christ. He wants us to cling to His promises that we will remain in His care even as we face these difficulties.

Here is what I know for sure:

- Nothing is random.
- God does nothing without a purpose.
- God chooses to do His will WITH us, not apart from us. We are part of His plan and purpose, not spectators.

God isn't one to inflict a tragedy like cancer or heart disease on His creation just to sit back and see how well we fare in the trial. Rather, He allows and orchestrates, in His sovereignty, things to come into our lives—often tragic events—and then blazes a trail for us to follow.

It's not about obedience or about the reward we might get in the hereafter. It's about bringing glory to the infinite, intelligent, personal Creator of the universe Who has a purpose for everything and everyone.

AFTERWORD

In June 2005, Christian underwent a catheter procedure to determine whether or not he was a candidate for the third surgery in his prescribed treatment, the Fontan. It was discovered that the pressures in the chambers of his heart were too high to go ahead with this surgery. A plan was considered to perform an intermediate surgery in October to reduce the pressures in Christian's heart. However, in early September, Christian went into congestive heart failure. Further surgery was out of the question.

After consulting with various cardiologists and cardiac surgeons, we decided to pursue a heart transplant for Christian. In late October, Christian was placed on the UNOS (United Network for Organ Sharing) list and came under the care of the transplant team at Lucile Packard Children's Hospital at Stanford.

On January 13, 2006, just five days after Christian's two younger brothers, Zacharias and Tobias, were born, we received a call from a transplant surgeon at Packard. They had located a heart and needed us to bring Christian to the hospital right away. After quite a few tests, Christian went into surgery to receive a new heart. After six weeks of recovery at Packard and another two at Ronald MacDonald House, Christian came home.

When the option of the heart transplant was presented to us, the team made it clear that we were trading one condition for another. Without a transplant, Christian's heart would fail and take his body with it. With a transplant, Christian would spend the rest of his life trying to keep his body from killing his new heart. And that has been the case.

In March 2009, Christian was diagnosed with posttransplant lymphoproliferative disorder (PTLD) triggered by the Epstein-Barr virus that Christian contracted the previous year. Four years later, the PTLD became Hodgkin's lymphoma. Christian spent 2014 undergoing chemotherapy and radiation treatment. In May 2015, his oncologist declared him in remission.

One year later, Christian was showing signs of a blood disease. His frequent bruising and bleeding issues were eventually diagnosed as idiopathic thrombocytopenic purpura or ITP. He continues to be under treatment for this condition.

Despite a number of medical hurdles, Christian has not only survived but thrived. At eighteen years old, he has never had any issues with his new heart. His visits to various specialists are far less frequent. He is physically active and excels at his schoolwork. He hopes to study graphic design and loves to spend time with his two older and two younger brothers.

We thank God every day for every day he has given us with Christian. We thank God for shaping us into the persons we are because He chose to bless us with this boy.

Printed in the United States
by Baker & Taylor Publisher Services